The
FAITH
of a
CHILD

A Step-by-Step Guide to
Salvation for your Child

ART MURPHY

MOODY PRESS
CHICAGO

All Scripture quotations, unless otherwise indicated, are taken from the *Holy Bible, New International Version®*. NIV®. Copyright © 1973, 1978, 1984 by International Bible Society. Used by permission of Zondervan Publishing House. All rights reserved.

Scripture quotations marked KJV are taken from the King James Version.

Library of Congress Cataloging-in-Publication Data

Murphy, Art.
    The faith of a child: a step-by-step guide to salvation for
    your child / Art Murphy. p. cm.
    ISBN 0-8024-5146-2
    1. Christian education of children. 2. Parenting—Religious
Aspects—Christianity. I. Title

BV1475.2 .M85 2000
248.8'45—dc21

5 7 9 10 8 6 4

Printed in the United States of America

The

FAITH
of a
CHILD

To my grandparents,
Dr. Slater A. Murphy Sr. and Mattie Elizabeth Murphy,
whose godly lives continue to impact my life

Contents

Introduction

*W*hen our boys were very young I heard them playing together one day, pretending that they were going to heaven. Ben asked Patrick, his younger brother, "How are we going to get there?"

Patrick answered, "There is a button that says 'up,' and you push it."

Children have all kinds of ideas on how to get to heaven, but this book is written to help you give clear direction to your children about how to go to heaven. This book is about helping children become Christians.

My main purpose for writing this book is not to place myself as the expert in the area of children and salvation, though I feel very confident about the information that will be presented. Hundreds of churches and thousands of parents and children's leaders have already found these lessons to be the help they needed. My main purpose is that parents and others who affect the lives of children will be better equipped and more confident to lead their children to a real relationship with Jesus.

We should not be too concerned about how or when God saves children. We don't have to worry about God doing His part. His timing is perfect. His plan is for children to come to Him. The focus of this book, however, is *our* part. We should concern ourselves more with the things we will do to help our children follow the Lord. We don't see things as completely as God does. We need help. And most of all, we do not want to do anything that would misguide or confuse children, and so prevent them from coming to the Lord.

Early in my service as a children's ministry pastor I realized that *most parents, teachers, and pastors struggle with the issue of children and salvation.* I struggled too. There are many questions to consider.

- How can we know if a child is ready to become a Christian?
- How much does a child have to know? How much should he understand?
- At what age are children mature enough to make this commitment?
- When should we start explaining the gospel to children?
- What must a child do to become a Christian?
- How much should we be involved in a child's decision?
- When should a child be baptized?
- What is the purpose of baptism?
- What can churches do to help raise children to follow the Lord?
- What help should churches provide for children who have expressed a desire to become Christians?
- Should the church leave a child's decision to become a Christian completely up to the child and his parents?
- What should we do when a very young child wants to become a Christian?

I will try to answer these and other questions. We will look at the stages of spiritual development—what happens at different ages from preschool to preteen. We will examine the signs that tell us whether a child is ready to become a Christian.

These are just a sampling of the questions we ask regarding children and salvation. They are good questions. We should concern ourselves with such questions when we are dealing with children. But God does not want us to be afraid, nervous, or worried. He wants us to be equipped and confident. He wants us to know His Word, to accept the responsibility He has given us for children, to understand children, and to trust Him to help us. Stop right now and ask God to help you as you continue reading. Ask Him to speak to you and show you how to better lead children to Him.

I have observed four changes or stages that occur in a child's life as he develops spiritually. These will be discussed later. Once we understand how children develop spiritually, we are much more aware of and sensitive to their needs. We know that preschoolers and preteens are very different. We should keep this in mind when we talk with children about Christ.

Discovering the different stages of spiritual development in children has helped me tremendously when talking to children about the Lord. This information has given me the confidence that is needed. It definitely opened my eyes to a better understanding of how children go from hearing the gospel to personally committing themselves to Christ. It has also given me some handles that have helped me develop age-appropriate witnessing approaches. Knowing these stages has helped thousands of parents and teachers build their confidence in discussing their faith with their children. That is exciting.

Have you noticed that when you are uncomfortable with something you tend to avoid it? Understanding the different characteristics of age, maturity, and spiritual development will encourage you to be more personally involved in the spiritual lives of children. You will become more effective. Plus, you will be able to teach and observe more appropriately. *However, know-*

ing this information only serves as a guide and should not take the place of your dependence on the Holy Spirit to help you. Nor should it take the place of knowing that individual child.

Our confidence in discussing with children how to become a Christian is strengthened when we better understand them. Our confidence is also strengthened when we let the Holy Spirit lead us. The same Holy Spirit who convicts us of our sin is also faithful to comfort us, teach us, and lead us when we need help. We must always rely on the leading of the Holy Spirit when discussing Christ with others, especially when we are talking with children. Depending on the Holy Spirit will help us become more sensitive to the needs of children. Asking the Holy Spirit to guide us will provide us with greater wisdom than we will have if we try to go it alone in our own strength.

In addition to being confident while communicating Christ to children, we must be available and usable. We must stay close to God through prayer and living a godly life. James 5:16 says, "The prayer of a righteous man is powerful and effective." First Peter 3:12 says, "For the eyes of the Lord are on the righteous and his ears are attentive to their prayer, but the face of the Lord is against those who do evil." What are the lessons here? God honors the prayers of the righteous. Keep yourself clean before God that He may use you. Pray for the children to whom you will be witnessing.

You will soon discover that, in most cases, *leading a child to Christ involves more than the few minutes it takes to lead him in the "sinner's prayer."* God wants your involvement to be far deeper. It will include your becoming more knowledgeable, sensitive, and patient as God does His complete work in that child's life. And, believe me, it will be worth it. My desire is that you become a messenger whom God will use to bring children into the kingdom of heaven. What could be more wonderful than that?

Leading a child to Christ is a journey. It is one that you must take with your child. The journey begins before he begins to ask questions about God. God is working before, during, and after a child's decision to become a Christian. Therefore, if possible, we should be involved in the child's spiritual life before, during, and after his decision.

We should not ignore a child's spiritual life while waiting for the child to initiate an interest. God uses us to help create that interest. We should start early in a child's life teaching him about the Lord. On the other hand, when a child begins to have an interest in God, we should not immediately lead him to ask the Lord into his life. We begin by feeding him spiritual milk until he can eat meat. Our goal should not be "How early can we get this child to make a decision to follow Christ?" Our goal should be "What can we do to help this child want to follow the Lord and make a lifelong commitment to Him?"

One Thanksgiving I decided to give my dog, Duke, a treat. I decided that, instead of his regular dog food, I would surprise him with the leftover turkey scraps. He practically inhaled all of it. It was obvious that he enjoyed every bite. But I made a big mistake by feeding Duke what I thought would be a treat. Instead, it made him sick. For two days his stomach was terribly upset. He was not ready for that type of food; his stomach could not digest it properly. He needed food that was specifically designed for him. For two days he suffered because of my good intentions.

We do not want to give children inappropriate spiritual food. We do not want to give them too much too soon or too little too late. If they need baby food, then we should give them baby food. If they are ready for a meatier diet, then we need to recognize that and know how to provide it. So often when we feed children spiritually we give them whatever we can think of, not knowing whether it is appropriate or not. We give them the scraps, the leftovers, and not the diet that they need. We cannot and should not witness to children the way we witness to adults and expect the same results. Initially, children may seem responsive or agreeable, but they probably will not be able to digest it all.

Psalm 127:4 says children are like *arrows*. Arrows are designed to hit targets, but they will never hit targets without the careful aim of a trained archer. We should desire to be accurate marksmen when it comes to aiming our children toward God. Our greatest fear is that we might miss the mark or fall short of the target. We can also miss by shooting past God if we are not careful. But our children's spiritual lives are so important that we cannot afford to miss. We only get the chance to aim our children while they are young. We must take our job as archers seriously. If we are not accurate, if we are off a few degrees, those arrows will be way off course later. This is why it is so important to know what our targets are and how to point our children toward God.

Many experts have noted that if children do not accept Christ before they are fourteen, then the chance of their ever becoming believers is greatly diminished. This is why we should not wait until our children address the subject with us. We should be the ones to originate the spiritual training. We should be the ones to introduce our kids to Jesus. We should begin teaching our children about God a long time before they are mature enough to become Christians.

Wouldn't it be helpful if we had more information about a child's spiritual development? Wouldn't it be fantastic if more parents, pastors, and teachers were prepared to help their children accept the Lord? Wouldn't it be a blessing if more of those who have the opportunity to influence the lives of children were involved in their children's conversion to Christianity and continual spiritual growth? That is what I hope will become your vision as you read this book.

Witnessing to children does not mean that you have memorized a gospel presentation and have the charisma to persuade a child to make a decision. Children can be easily persuaded. Witnessing to a child begins with knowing how to take his spiritual temperature. It means that you are wise in discerning what that child's spiritual needs are. It means that you are sensitive to what he is capable of understanding and applying to his life.

Prepare yourself so that you can become involved in helping your children with this decision. Please do not do what so many do during this precious part of their children's lives—do not leave them all alone with their decision to follow Christ. Leaving this decision totally up to children leaves them vulnerable targets for the Enemy.

Even if a child says all of the right things, he may not be ready to accept Christ. Even if he is very anxious (or impatient) to become a Christian, this does not guarantee that he is ready. On the other hand, he may find it difficult to express himself but have real conviction in his heart. A child who has never experienced salvation does not know what to expect and should not be abandoned while making this decision. He needs you to help him. Though you cannot make his decision for him, he does need your guidance with this. Do not leave his decision up to chance. Feel free to jump right in and get involved.

A shepherd does not ignore his little lambs so he can give greater care to the older sheep. He does not send the lambs out alone to face the wild animals and harmful elements. He gives his lambs extra special care, never letting them out of his sight. The shepherd's staff is there to direct the lambs and to fight off attackers. Sometimes the shepherd will have to hook a lamb in his crook and pull it away from the cliff, because the lamb does not see what lies ahead.

We must take the same approach with *our* little lambs. We should not let them journey alone in their decision to follow Christ. The decision is too important, and so are they. We cannot let them out of our sight. Even adults get confused about what it means to become a Christian. And children are not strong or wise. They cannot make this decision alone. They need our love and leadership. They are our lambs. A good shepherd knows his flock and protects his lambs.

When I was about twelve, my dad asked me to go with him and some other men on a hunting trip. I was excited. I knew how to shoot and was educated in all the gun safety rules. I had already been hunting on several occasions, most of them close to home. But this trip was for men (not boys) who were serious hunters. We hunted all day for two or three days. The trip involved lots of walking, climbing, and wading. To my surprise, my little weak legs could not take it. Early in the trip, my dad had to stop and carry me because I just could not keep up with him and the other men. Parents and teachers must carry their children until they are strong enough to walk unassisted. When discussing our faith with children, we do not give them more than they can carry (comprehend). We give them bits at a time. We help them build their faith. A house built on the sand will not stand, but a house built on the rock will withstand anything.

The faith of a child is a journey. Leading the children you influence to Jesus is not a one-time event. It is a great privilege for me to speak to you about such a precious topic. Thanks for allowing me to walk alongside you in this journey and point you in some directions that will help you direct your children. My desire is that this study will help you become better equipped, more relaxed, and more effective. My prayer is that you will be blessed and encouraged and find this book to be a help to you and the children you touch.

I am very excited about explaining what God has shown me regarding children and salvation. I hope you will be blessed by what you are about to discover. You will learn what you can do to prepare yourself for the moment God begins to speak to your child. Besides the encouragement and confidence you will receive, I will be telling you some practical ideas that will help you better understand children and how they come to know the Lord.

Our responsibility as adults is to lead children in the right direction. Psalm 127:3–5 says, "Sons are a heritage from the Lord, children a reward from him. Like arrows in the hands of a warrior are sons born in one's youth. Blessed is the man whose quiver is full of them." Children are God's gift to us, a blessing to our lives. I am thankful to God for calling me to pastor children, allowing me to touch the lives of children. They have blessed my life. I am also thankful that He has allowed me the privilege and opportunity to encourage you who affect the lives of boys and girls. The faith of a child is a precious thing. Join me now as we look at the faith of a child.

Chapter One
Building a Strong Spiritual Foundation for Your Child

During my childhood our family built a home. It was exciting driving out each day to see what had been accomplished since the day before. Construction still fascinates me. It amazes me how buildings start from just ideas and then end up as remarkable structures. I enjoy watching the planners, architects, and builders work together to accomplish their goal. Each one is important to the construction process. To me this is art in motion, from the initial design to the completed structure.

God has given us the awesome blessing and responsibility of helping Him build the lives of our children. This is the greatest construction of all. If we are going to build a strong spiritual foundation in a child's life, we will first need to know God's plan, His blueprint. Next, we begin by laying a solid foundation. We would never consider living in a house that had no foundation or a weak one. The first storm that came along would wipe it out. Neither would we knowingly buy a house from a builder who had hurried the construction or used materials of poor quality.

Have you ever taken a tour of a movie production lot? Did you see the beautifully constructed houses with perfectly manicured lawns? You probably were shown that these structures are not houses at all. They are only facades. They are built to give the appearance of houses, but in fact they are just props. They have no backs, insides, plumbing, or foundations. They are fake houses.

Do you see the lesson here? Children who are taught to act or talk like Christians without actually becoming Christians are not Christians. Children can give the appearance of being Christians because they have learned all the right information. However, that does not make them Christians. What is built on the inside is more important than what can be seen from the outside. The spiritual foundation we lay for a child's life is what the Holy Spirit will use when the child begins to become a Christian. It is the foundation on which he will build his whole Christian life.

In Jesus' day some men gave the appearance of belonging to God, but He saw right through them and called them "hypocrites." Help your child see the difference between knowing about Jesus and actually following Jesus. You not only want your child to know the definition of sin, but you also want him to truly repent of his sin. Help your child have a strong and personal faith in Christ by building a solid Christian foundation.

Good building blocks will help you build a solid spiritual foundation in your child's life. They are the greatest gifts you can give a child. Building a strong spiritual foundation for your child will prepare his heart for the Holy Spirit's conviction and leading. It will protect him from enemy arrows (fear, confusion, false teachings, temptation, pride, etc.). It will help him become a solid Christian.

BUILDING BLOCKS FOR A CHILD'S FAITH

A Godly Home

Whether your home has two parents, a single parent, or a blended family, you can have a Christian home, but it takes work. It takes work even when both parents are Christians. There are no shortcuts. Why? Parenting is hard work. Furthermore, Satan attacks parents, and he attacks children. But there is good news. God wants us to have healthy family relationships, strong marriages, and obedient children, which equal happy homes. However, this is not possible unless we invite God to be in charge of our families. When the presence of God is evident in parents' lives, their children are drawn to follow Christ with their lives. Christians who live faithful, obedient, joyful, disciplined, and godly lives affect those with whom they come in contact. Our impact as Christian parents is even more powerful. God wants parents to be the most influential shapers of their children's spiritual lives.

The characteristics that we possess influence what characteristics our children will possess. Our personalities help form their personalities. Our outlook and attitude shape theirs. Whether or not parents are Christians, they influence their children's spiritual lives. If you take the approach of leaving it up to the church to develop your children's spiritual life, you are making a gigantic mistake.

However, the church can and should come alongside the family. God has used many wonderful church leaders who teach children in Sunday school, vacation Bible school, church camp, Christian school, and other settings and who influence the lives of children in a tremendous way. These people are a parent's spiritual teammates. Parents should express heartfelt appreciation to those who affect their children for Christ.

Leading childhood educators and psychologists have told us for many years that a child's adult personality is about 90 percent complete by the age of five. This is another reason we should start a child's spiritual training from the time he or she is born. Spiritual training is not just sitting down with your child each week or each night to discuss the things of God. Having scheduled times for Bible stories, devotions, and discussion is very important. But a godly home is more than that. A godly home has an atmosphere. It has an attitude. It has purpose.

What is a godly home? A godly home begins with each parent being a committed Christian. The parents must also be committed to their marriage. All other family relationships are built from this most important relationship. Children watch the relationship between their parents and use it as a measuring stick for other relationships. Through their parents' example, children learn trust, patience, forgiveness, unselfishness, dependence, commitment, and love. By watching their parents' love for each other and for God, children learn about God. Marriage demonstrates to the children whether or not we really mean what we say about God.

Do not make the mistake that many couples make when they have children. They elevate the role of parent higher than that of spouse. This creates a home that is off-balance and will be greatly challenged when problems and stresses from life come along. God's Word teaches that a Christian home is made up of two godly parents involved in raising their children. The husband/father has specific duties, and so does the wife/mother. When these roles are ignored, overlooked, forgotten, or neglected, then chaos occurs.

If you are a single parent or a parent married to a nonbeliever, then you may at times feel very much alone. But you can be assured that God is with you and will use your influence in your children's lives even when you do not have anyone else supporting your efforts. It is also important, when you do not have a Christian partner at home, to build a team of Christian supporters around you and your children—church leaders, teachers, coaches, and relatives, to name a few. Ask them to be spiritual helpers, guides, advisers, and encouragers to you and your children.

The type of home a person has during childhood affects him for the rest of his life. Here is an example of how the present Sunday school attendance of parents influences the future Sunday school attendance of their children. Research shows that

• When *both parents* attend Sunday school, 72 percent of the children attend Sunday school when grown.

- When *only the father* attends Sunday school, 55 percent of the children attend when grown.
- When *only the mother* attends Sunday school, 15 percent of the children attend when grown.
- When *neither parent* attends Sunday school, only 6 percent of the children attend when grown.[1]

Meaningful Relationships

Jesus taught us about relationships. Not only did He teach us that our relationship with God was supreme, but He also taught us that our relationships with others are very important. One way Christians should show the world the difference Christ makes in their lives is through their relationships with others. Christians are honest. Christians are servants. Christians forgive. Christians apologize. Christians give instead of taking. Christians speak the truth in love. Christians build others up instead of tearing them down. Christians love people.

Children are born self-centered and must be taught to share, consider others' feelings, work together, make friends, keep friends, and get along with others. How do they learn about relationships? They watch our relationships. They watch the way we treat our own parents, siblings, friends, neighbors, colleagues, employers, employees, the elderly, the wealthy, the less fortunate, and even strangers.

Families in general are so busy that they don't make time to make friends. Children too are so busy that they do not spend time developing friendships as they should. Friendships take time. And often children do not know how to make them. Give your children lessons in making friends by having people in your home. Invite relatives, neighbors, and friends from church to your home.

Not only do children learn about God by watching our Christianity through our relationships; they are also influenced by our behavior in everyday life situations. They listen to us when we get upset in traffic, they watch our actions at Little

League games and sporting events, and they see what we watch on TV. We can tell our children about Jesus, but the old saying is still true: "Actions speak louder than words."

Good Habits

When we help children develop good habits, we shape their personality, character, and behavior. Children who are taught good habits (and who observe them) are more likely to be teachable in general. Children who are submissive to parental authority find it easier to submit to God's authority. Children who are not raised to be submissive to parental authority will find it tougher to submit to other authorities in their lives such as teachers, pastors, employers, and even God.

Teaching children good habits is an important part of disciplining them. So we teach them to brush their teeth, do chores, do homework, exercise, read, straighten their rooms, show respect to parents and other adults through speech and actions, write thank-you notes, read the Bible, etc. Discipline teaches children to be good decision makers. Discipline teaches children to be under control instead of being out of control. Disciplined children are better time managers and better money managers. Disciplined children are stronger than other children when faced with a temptation. Children who are disciplined are stronger, happier, better adjusted, better leaders, and better achievers. Disciplined athletes win championships. Disciplined children win at life.

Deciding to raise disciplined children means that you as the adult must also be disciplined. You cannot expect to raise children who are disciplined if you are not disciplined. If you have bad habits in your life, there is a greater chance that your children will have those bad habits too.

Let your children see that you too are striving to be better disciplined. Let them see your victories and failures. Strive for excellence but allow for failure. Teach your children how to handle failure. Failure can be defeating if we do not know how to handle it. If you are too rigid, then your children will not experience grace, and you will raise legalistic children, not disciplined children.

Raising disciplined children does not mean taking away their personalities. Neither does it mean taking away their joy. We do not want our children to become robots. Society sometimes defines a disciplined life as a life with too many restraints and not enough fun. A rigid, legalistic approach to discipline can leave that impression with our children. A disciplined home should also be a fun home with plenty of room for each child's God-given personality and talents to be appreciated, developed, and enjoyed.

However, a child raised with no discipline finds it difficult adjusting to the real adult world of responsibility. To live a disciplined life is to live a balanced life. Living a disciplined life means getting one's life in order by setting priorities and striving to reach them. Children who are disciplined are more sensitive and appreciative of values. They also tend to weigh the consequences of their actions, good and bad, therefore making better decisions.

Becoming a Christian involves choosing Christian values, decision making, living a balanced life, and striving for excellence. It also teaches us about how to deal with failure. None of us can ever be good enough to be a Christian, but once we say "yes" to God's authority in our lives, He begins to shape us and we begin to develop habits in our lives that bring ultimate joy. Becoming a Christian is about freedom, not bondage. It is about living life to the fullest, not just constant sacrifice. Give your children a head start toward being sensitive to the Holy Spirit by teaching them to be sensitive to your authority. Lead your children to be disciplined. Teach them good habits.

Paul Lewis, formerly the editor of *Dads Only* magazine, wrote that the two greatest gifts to give your children are "good habits and good memories."

A Positive Attitude About Life and God
Chuck Swindoll wrote this about attitude:

Words can never adequately convey the incredible impact of our attitude toward life. The longer I live the more convinced I become that life is 10 percent what happens to us and 90 percent how we respond to it.

I believe the single most significant decision I can make on a day-to-day basis is my choice of attitude. It is more important than my past, my education, my bankroll, my successes or failures, fame or pain, what other people think of me or say about me, my circumstances, or my position. Attitude keeps me going or cripples my progress. It alone fuels my fire or assaults my hope. When my attitudes are right, there's no barrier too high, no valley too deep, no dream too extreme, no challenge too great for me.[2]

Christians are not losers; they are not defeated. Therefore, they should not have defeated or negative attitudes. Christians are victorious and should have winning attitudes. Avoid worrying. Stop being critical of everything and everyone. Quit wasting your precious energy on things that are not productive. Be positive about life and what God is doing in your life. Teach your children to be positive, constructive, and victorious. Christians who whine, complain, judge, fight, and criticize are not very attractive to the world. They are not very appealing to children either. Show your children that Christians really can and do have more fun. Make sure that your children see you smile and hear you laugh every day.

Godly Role Models and Heroes

Good heroes will add character and quality to your children's lives. But good heroes can sometimes be hard to find. Where can a parent go to find positive heroes for his or her children?

God uses the lives of godly men and women to affect the lives of others, especially children. God's people should have a natural attractiveness. Because of the positive characteristics demonstrated in Christians' lives, others around them are drawn to seek God. The world is looking for good moral role models.

Who are your children's heroes? Who are your heroes? Do they point children to God, or do they point them to the world, away from God?

Children do not know the differences between a hero and an idol. An idol is an image (something or someone) that man (Hollywood, television, sports, movies, etc.) has created to worship. It is fake. A hero is someone we admire for the qualities that are evident in his life. A hero is real. Children are so easily influenced that they are often deceived. They tend to get caught up in idol worship due to the hype often associated with it. Children need us to help them select good heroes, mentors, and examples for their lives.

It is difficult for children (and adults for that matter) to resist the media hype that is pushed on them. Millions of dollars are spent in convincing children to choose certain images, toys, games, products, movie stars, and athletes in order to be considered valuable or cool by their peers. Wise parents help guide their children away from this pressure. Wise parents expose their children to good men and women who will add value to their lives. These heroes are sometimes hard to find, but they do exist. By helping your children choose the right Christian examples, you are helping them see the difference that Christ makes in people's lives. You are giving them spiritual direction.

Remember, Christians are not perfect, and neither are your children's heroes. Even heroes fail from time to time. This is disappointing to children when it happens. When it does, use it to show your children that none of us is perfect. We all need Christ as our master, no matter who we are or how famous we are.

Open Communication

Developing open communication with your children means that you will have to spend time with them. Are you too busy to talk to your children? Do they ask questions at the most inconvenient times? Do you tell them "just a minute" and then forget to check back to see what their questions were? Do they ask questions that you cannot answer? Do they ask so many questions at once that you get tired of hearing them?

Sometimes the only time children can get their parents' *undivided* attention is when they ask their parents questions about God. Encourage your children to discuss their feelings with you and to ask questions. Talk about lots of topics. Respond to your children when they ask questions. Take advantage of times when your children are in a talking mood. Teach them the value of talking. Use the precious time you have to get to know your children and develop open lines of communication. Parents should spend at least fifteen minutes each day talking with each of their children. Teachers should periodically call their students just to talk.

How well do you know your children? The more time you spend talking with them, the better you will know your children and the better they will know you. Good communication skills help you and your children learn how to discuss problems, ask questions, correct misunderstandings, become more sensitive to others, listen, interpret body language, and express yourselves. Communication skills are such a help when you are trying to understand how (or if) God is working in your children's lives. Good communication is the first step toward building trust.

All of us, not just children, have questions about the things of God. And that is not wrong. Our questions can be His magnet for greater discoveries about Him. It is very important that you create an atmosphere with your children in which questions are invited, not avoided.

THE CHURCH'S ROLE IN A CHILD'S FAITH

The church should not be a substitute for the parents' role as the spiritual leaders in their children's lives. However, the Bible tells us that we are to faithfully assemble together as a body of believers. We are to participate in worship and Bible teaching.

As Christians we each have different spiritual gifts, and we each make up a part of the body of Christ. We need each other. We are taught to minister to others and encourage one another. We meet to learn, grow, pray, confess, share, give, sing, praise, and so forth. We don't just *go* to church. We *are* the church. We need to assemble each week in order to keep our focus as a body of believers. When we do not meet regularly, we become disjointed and weak. Faithful church attendance is important to your spiritual health and that of your children.

Do you hate it when you hear your children use the "b" word? Me too. I hate it when I hear children say that their experience at church or Sunday school was "boring." Church should be the highlight of the week for you and your children. One of the worst influences on your child is to attend a spiritually dead church. If the church you attend is spiritually dead, pray about moving. Find one that is alive in its worship and Bible study. Look for a church that has children's activities that are fun, productive, and spiritually alive.

The term "fun" is not to indicate that children will always love going to church or want to do what they are taught. The focus is on a healthy church, one that realizes the importance of a children's ministry and seeks to improve how it teaches and ministers to children. "Fun" does not mean that a church must have a carnival atmosphere. The Bible contains the most interesting, intriguing, life-changing stories of any book. If we really want to reach children with the gospel, then we should evaluate our methods and seek ways to improve our teaching. A fun Sunday school class is one that is Bible centered, uses a variety of learning styles (hands-on activities, not just lecture), chooses curriculum that is age-appropriate, and is led by enthusiastic adults who love the Lord and children. Fun classrooms use music and games for learning. Fun classrooms allow children to ask questions. Fun classrooms have teachers who smile and laugh and hug. Fun classrooms are classrooms that make children say, "I can't wait until next Sunday."

You can help your child have a positive experience at church. Personally get involved in your children's activities at church. Just think how much more open your children will be to spiritual things when they are excited about attending and seeing you excited too. But be aware. The Enemy will do everything he can to keep you and your children from finding and attending a good church.

I thank God for dedicated men and women who love children and teach them about Jesus. Many boys and girls would not be part of God's family if it were not for the wonderful teachers who have touched their lives. If you teach children about Jesus, I thank you. You have a special place in my heart. You probably do not receive the public recognition that you deserve, though you are not doing what you do for recognition. You are about the King's business. On behalf of every parent and pastor let me say, "You are one of the most important parts in the body of Christ." Teach others how to do what you do, and don't ever lose your passion for reaching children for Christ.

NOTES

1. Quoted in Sid Woodruff, *Drawing Men to God,* from Robert and Debra Bruce, *Becoming Spiritual Soulmates with Your Child* (Broadman & Holman, 1996), 52.

2. Charles R. Swindoll, *Strengthening Your Grip* (Nashville: Word, 1982). All rights reserved. Used by permission of Insight for Living, Anaheim, California 92806.

Chapter Two

What God Says About Children and Salvation

$\mathcal{M}$ost people who have been Christians for a while know what the Bible says about salvation. They probably can quote John 3:16 by heart or are familiar with certain verses from the book of Romans. However, it gets a bit trickier when they try to think of Scriptures that relate to children. Does the Bible say anything about children and salvation? Most of us struggle trying to recall such Scriptures. Actually, the Bible says some precious things about children and gives parents great guidance in leading their children to follow the Lord. Let's look at what the Bible says.

WHAT DOES THE BIBLE SAY ABOUT CHILDREN?

Children Are a Gift from the Lord

Psalm 127:3 says, "Sons are a heritage from the Lord, children a reward from him." I have been reminded all throughout our boys' lives that they truly are gifts from God. One day, during a meeting in my office, I received a phone call. I knew that it must be important since my secretary knew not to interrupt me. It was my wife, Lois Ann. When I answered, the first words she said were "Art, Patrick is OK, but he has just been hit by a car." That was a devastating moment. I felt a hurt that I cannot describe. I almost lost one of the dearest and most important people in my life . . . my youngest son. I was helpless. I had to totally trust God with this.

For the next forty-five minutes I waited in agony until I received my wife's second call telling me where the ambulance had taken Patrick. My prayer at that time was "God, please protect my son, and let me see him alive." I knew God was in control, but I was dying inside. This event reminded me how brief life is and that I am not guaranteed that my children will live a certain number of years. They are a gift on loan from God.

Patrick was six years old when this happened. He was hit while walking his bike in a crosswalk. An elderly gentleman accidentally ran a traffic light, striking Patrick and throwing him up onto the sidewalk. Patrick suffered a broken collarbone, scrapes and bruises, mild shock, and a demolished bike.

That was several years ago, but I remember it like it was yesterday. Each time I go by that intersection I thank God for sparing Patrick's life. God richly blessed us when He gave us Ben and Patrick. They are truly gifts from the Lord.

Children Are Easily Influenced and Directed

Psalm 127:4 tells us, "Like arrows in the hands of a warrior are sons born in one's youth."

Parenting is a lot like archery. During the first round we get a few shots up close. At the next round the target is moved farther away. This continues until the target is almost out of sight. As parents we should take advantage of the opportunity we have while our children are young, while they are easily influenced. When they become teenagers our role as parents changes. It changes again when our children go off to college, move away, become adults, or get married. Our influence is distanced.

As a warrior provides protection for his family and city, we should protect our children. We should provide a strong Christian influence in their lives and aim them toward their own personal relationship with God. Our arrows, our children, should be cared for, equipped, and properly aimed. We hold their direction, their future, in our hands.

You are a marksman who only gets one shot. Once your arrow has been released into the world, it is on its own. You cannot stop it. Cherish your arrows. Sharpen your arrows. Aim them toward Christ. No one influences a child like his parents do. Be the warrior, the archer for Christ that your children need.

Children Are Responsive and Sensitive to the Things of God

In Matthew 11:25 Jesus said, "I praise you, Father, Lord of heaven and earth, because you have hidden these things from the wise and learned, and revealed them to little children."

Jesus refers to children (or babes) to help make an important point. The term *children* refers to those who are humble, who realize their helplessness, as opposed to the wise, who think they know it all or have reached a level of self-accomplishment and don't need God. Jesus not uses this Scripture to teach us about our need to be open to Him, but He also reminds us that children have some unique characteristics. Children are teachable, dependent, obedient, trusting, faithful, responsive, absorbent, accepting, loyal, submissive, and sensitive, to name a few. Though children are born with a sinful nature, they can be easily led and influenced for God.

Our children's ministry began a new program at the beginning of the year 2000 to help children develop good habits such as faithful Sunday school attendance, bringing their Bible, staying for worship, bringing a friend, etc. We called it "M & M 2000." M & M stood for "My Master and Me." To motivate the kids we gave points for each category. This became a fun way to teach them some basic habits of the Christian life.

As one of our third-grade directors was explaining all of the details to his class, a little boy raised his hand, and with excitement in his voice he asked, "Do we get more points if the visitor we bring decides to become a Christian?" This young man may not have received more points during that special program, but I guarantee that God rewards children who are sensitive to Him and want to bring their friends to the Lord.

Another Sunday morning during the Easter season, a teacher was telling the Easter story to her second-grade Sunday school class. One of her boys, the biggest and most active in the class, was on the edge of his seat. As soon as she finished, his hand shot up in the air. Without waiting to be called on to speak, he blurted out, "Miss Shirley, Miss Shirley, we have to tell everybody." He had never heard that story. He thought that it had just happened that weekend. The Good News is still good, and it is still news. And children are eager to respond. I am so glad that God let me be in Miss Shirley's class that very special day.

The faith of a child is so precious. It puts our faith to shame. A child's faith is also very vulnerable. Children need help with their faith. The Bible speaks about a parent's responsibility in raising a child of faith. I believe that God's Word teaches us to spend the childhood years in teaching, modeling, and discipling. It is tempting at times to skip that stage of parenting because it can be very demanding and even puzzling at times. But spiritual training calls for great patience on our part.

Jesus Loved Children and Made Time for Them

The Bible says in Mark 10:16 that Jesus "took the children in his arms, put his hands on them and blessed them."

I don't recall His taking the disciples in His arms like this. He took children in His arms. He could have just spoken to those children. He could have given them some sort of gift to appease them. He could have chosen to have a question-and-answer time with them. He could have asked the disciples to provide child care for them while He spoke with their parents. He could have told His disciples to send them away because He was too busy. But He didn't. He took them in His arms and blessed them.

Jesus' acceptance of these children speaks volumes. His recognition and acceptance of children demonstrated how valuable children are to Him. You can be assured that Jesus wants to take children in His arms. He wants them from a young age to be close to Him. He wants them to feel free to come to Him, to observe Him, and not to be afraid of Him. He wants children to love Him.

Matthew 19:13–14 tells the same story about Jesus and the children. It gives us an example of Jesus' great love for children. "Then little children were brought to Jesus for him to place his hands on them and pray for them. But the disciples rebuked those who brought them. Jesus said, 'Let the little children come to me, and do not hinder them, for the kingdom of heaven belongs to such as these.'"

These Scriptures are often misused as prime examples of "child evangelism." Jesus was not emphasizing that we should evangelize infants and little children. He was showing us how much He loved them. He was elevating their value in society and His kingdom. As a matter of fact, He pointed out that they already have a place in the kingdom. These children and infants were under the age of knowing right from wrong. They were not old enough to be "lost." They were not yet in need of salvation. They were safe . . . safe in His arms. Jesus' ministry to children was different from His ministry to adults. His role was to hug and bless children. He left the responsibility of spiritual training up to the parents.

Jesus knew that the greatest impact for evangelism that He could have on these young children was to love them, teach them, and bless them. These young children were not ready to be born again; they had barely been born once. Jesus took every opportunity to bring the lost to Himself. Knowing the needs of children, He approached them appropriately.

Jesus did warn us that we are *not to hinder young children*. If we hinder (hold back, interfere, obstruct) them when they are young, they may not want to come to Christ later when they are mature enough to become Christians. If we acknowledge the value of young children and encourage and teach them from the time they are infants, they will be drawn to the Savior. We are to lead children to Jesus. The disciples rejected them because they did not see the value in children that Jesus saw.

Jesus Raised the Importance of Children

At the beginning of the eighteenth chapter of Matthew, Jesus called a little child to stand in His midst while He spoke. He used children as an example of greatness because of their genuine humility and innocence. Then in Matthew 18:10, 14 He said, "See that you do not look down on one of these little ones. For I tell you that their angels in heaven always see the face of my Father in heaven. . . . Your Father in heaven is not willing that any of these little ones should be lost." The disciples treated these children as unimportant to the Lord. Jesus treated them as the most important.

Jesus knew that they were at a very influential time when their spiritual lives were about to be shaped. Spending adequate time influencing, teaching, and feeding children will guard them from being lost. That is the responsibility we have with our young children.

It is not unusual for a child who is raised in a Christian home to want to become a Christian at an early age. I have known children as young as two years old who asked their parents about becoming a Christian. Even though statistics show that only 1 percent of decisions to accept Christ are made during the preschool years, my experience is that many of us struggle with this. Parents struggle because they know their children do not fully understand at this age, but they do not want to be a stumbling block by holding them back. Pastors also struggle when young children make decisions, but they do not want to upset the child or the parents. But most important, children struggle too.

If you struggle with the age issue, I want to help. My experience has been that most adults who made a decision as a young child (at the age of seven or younger) later had serious doubts about that decision, or made another decision years later to make sure.

Here is how we can help today's children. We definitely want to start while our children are young teaching them about Jesus and His plan for their lives. Because children are so tender, impressionable, and easily led to Jesus, we must be gentle and patient. We should not treat them as adults. We must realize that they need time to understand and grow. We must be as committed to helping children grow and mature as we are to leading them to make the decision to follow Christ. Most children come to understand what it means to become a Christian after they have stated that they want to become one. Their faith is so ready to trust Christ. Their eagerness is such a lesson to all of us. We should feed their faith. Sometimes we get so caught up with nailing down their decision that we miss the joy of feeding their faith. The "feeding" time is just as important as the "leading" (decision) time.

We Should Take Our Responsibility for Children Seriously

We should do all that we can to reach children with the good news that God loves them. In Matthew 18:5–6 Jesus said, "And whoever welcomes a little child like this in my name welcomes me. But if anyone causes one of these little ones who believe in me to sin, it would be better for him to have a large millstone hung around his neck and to be drowned in the depths of the sea."

We ache at the thought of someone intentionally causing an innocent child to sin. Anyone who would do something so hideous should be severely punished. But we can unintentionally cause a child to sin by just ignoring him. We should not wait to begin teaching children about God. We should teach children when they are very young that God has a plan for their lives.

The church should be a place where children feel welcomed, loved, encouraged, accepted, and happy. Churches should do everything possible to create a "child friendly" atmosphere.

Parents Should Teach Their Children About God

Deuteronomy 6:4–7 commands,

The LORD our God, the LORD is one. Love the LORD your

God with all your heart and with all your soul and with all your strength. These commandments that I give you today are to be upon your hearts. Impress them on your children. Talk about them when you sit at home and when you walk along the road, when you lie down and when you get up.

Notice that verse 7 says that we are to "impress" upon our children the teachings of God's Word. Impress means to mark, brand, mold, impact, influence, teach, love, lead, and disciple our children. This impression is similar to that we see in fossils. The mark that is made lasts for a lifetime and beyond. God's Word is serious about our responsibility to raise children to know Him.

It is our duty and privilege to pass our faith on to the next generation. Psalm 78:4 says, "We will tell the next generation the praiseworthy deeds of the LORD, his power, and the wonders he has done."

The Church Should Reach Men, Women, and Children

Deuteronomy 31:12–13 says,

> Gather the people together, men, and women, and *children,* and thy stranger that is within thy gates, that they may hear, and that they may learn, and fear the Lord your God, and observe to do all the words of this law: and that their *children,* which have not known any thing, may hear, and learn to fear the Lord your God. (KJV, italics added)

Biblical evangelism does not mean only that we are to go across the world to win people to Christ. Evangelism begins at home, then reaches out to our communities, then goes to other parts of the world. Proper evangelism cannot ignore our own children. We cannot assume that children are going to be saved just by attending church. Churches are full of children who have not accepted Christ as Savior and Lord. Churches need to have a strategy that includes winning their children to Christ. We must teach our children to fear the Lord. Too often the children are overlooked and we miss one of the most reachable groups closest to us.

Someone once said, "The greatest thing you can do for a child is to lead his parents to Christ." That assumes that the parents then establish a Christian home and teach their children about Christ.

WHAT DOES THE BIBLE SAY ABOUT THE AGE OF SALVATION?

We Are Sinful from Birth

Psalm 51:5 says, "Surely I have been a sinner from birth, sinful from the time my mother conceived me."

Parents are afraid that if one of their children dies at an early age he might not go to heaven. Because of that fear, parents are often scared into leading their children into premature decisions. Yet we cannot make this decision for our children. They must make it for themselves.

If you are a parent and you have a young child who has not accepted Christ, do not be afraid. Do not rush him to make this decision. If you lead him to become a Christian before he is mature enough to understand, he will think that he is a Christian when he is not.

Remember, God wants your child in His kingdom more than you do. But God's plan is usually one of order and growth. It unfolds a step at a time. He wants you to spend adequate time teaching your child about God. He wants you to have the joy of watching your child grow into a strong and meaningful relationship with Him. He does not want you to harm your child by rushing him in this decision. He wants you to lead him.

When Infants and Young Children Die, They Go to Heaven

Second Samuel 12:23 tells of the time when David lost an infant son. After much grief as the child was dying, David came to a place of peace with his death, for he knew that one day he would see his son again, that he would "go to him." Children too young to be "saved" are indeed "safe."

Children Are Childish and Immature

The apostle Paul said, "When I was a child, I talked like a child, I thought like a child, I reasoned like a child. When I became a man, I put childish ways behind me" (1 Corinthians 13:11). We should not treat children like little adults. Though they are highly intelligent beings, they are still children. We need to allow them to be children, though they may sound like adults sometimes. We should not get upset when they do not understand or they get confused. They need our patience.

Salvation Is the Same for Children and for Adults

Romans 10:9 says, "If you confess with your mouth, 'Jesus is Lord,' and believe in your heart that God raised him from the dead, you will be saved." Salvation is not one way for children and another way for adults. There is not a set of "junior rules" for children. Actually, salvation may be *the first "adult" decision* a child makes. He puts away his faith in childish things (fairy tales, Santa Claus, make-believe) and puts his trust in the reality and personal relationship of Jesus.

Please be careful how you use Scripture. Sometimes we twist Scripture to say what we want it to say. Matthew 18:3–4 says, "I tell you the truth, unless you change and become like little children, you will never enter the kingdom of heaven. Therefore, whoever humbles himself like this child is the greatest in the kingdom of heaven." This verse is often misquoted as illustrating the importance of evangelizing children. Really it is a message for adults about "greatness." Humility is a characteristic of greatness, and Jesus used a child to illustrate humility. Children can be so teachable, sensitive, honest, and humble. But although children are easily led and they respond quickly, we do not want them to skip any part of the salvation experience.

Jesus gives another example of how we can achieve greatness in the kingdom of heaven. He tells us in Matthew 18:5 that we are great when we welcome children in His name. This story contains many lessons. Here are a few:

- what type of person can enter the kingdom of heaven
- the attitude we should have in coming to Christ
- the importance of bringing others to Christ
- that we can come as we are to Christ
- that Christ does not refuse those who come to Him

Christians have many differing views on the topic of children and salvation. I have spoken with parents who believed their two-year-olds had "prayed the prayer." Others have felt that because their child "still sins" he is not *qualified* for salvation. Some do not think a child can be saved until the age of twelve. Others think it does not matter what we do. They believe that if God has chosen children to become Christians, then they will become Christians no matter what. So they do nothing to help. Some churches practice the baptism of babies almost as an act of salvation. None of these examples is supported by Scripture.

Since the Bible does not give us examples of children becoming Christians, we must be careful. We must know what the Bible says about children. Here is some of what it says.

- Jesus loves children.
- Jesus rebuked the disciples for trying to send children away.
- Jesus warned anyone who caused them to stumble.
- God commands parents to teach their children His ways.
- Jesus used the faith of children as an example for us.
- Children can believe in Jesus.

Can children be saved? Yes, they can. A large percent of the Christian population point to a time in their childhood years (fourteen and under) when their conversion took place.

Because the Bible does not say much about children becoming Christians, we tend to struggle when trying to involve children in spiritual training. Our struggles are demonstrated when we

- *neglect* children—ignore or forget about them, not taking them very seriously
- *abuse* children—respond inappropriately, taking Scriptures out of context, treating them like adults, using guilt or force, or expecting too much from them
- are *confused* about what to say or do with children
- are *afraid* or become nervous when we try to talk to children about salvation

Jesus used children as examples. He used children to teach us about faith, greatness, humility, and God's love. He encouraged us to welcome them as if we were welcoming Him. He warned us to avoid doing anything that would cause children who believe in Him to sin. We can conclude that children are very important to God.

Chapter Three

How Much Do You Know About Today's Children?

*C*hildren have not changed. Childhood has changed.

During 1999 an international scare arose due to the fact that computers were not programmed to read any date past 1999, which could cause them to crash on the first day of the year 2000. The world as we now know it could no longer exist. Communication relying on technology could cease. Power plants could fail. Law enforcement could be limited. Water could no longer be available. Never before has the whole world worked together so hard on one project. Billions of dollars were spent in studying this problem and upgrading the systems that were lacking in the proper technology. Thanks to all of the "debugging" that took place, the Y2K bug did little damage.

But another harmful "bug" still exists. This bug has practically gone unnoticed, but it is more damaging than a potential computer crash. It is a bug that exists in the lives of our children. Kids of the new millennium are being "bugged" by several negative forces that could destroy or greatly harm their childhood. They are doomed to "crash" unless we protect them from the harmful "viruses" that are attacking their spiritual lives. They are being robbed of their innocence and their childhood right before our eyes. They are being influenced to believe the philosophies of the world and reject the truths of God. If we are going to successfully reach today's child with the good news of Jesus, we must have a correct understanding of what this child faces and what he looks like. What are the influences in his life? How does he think? How is his childhood different from our childhood?

UNDERSTANDING TODAY'S CHILD

Here are some characteristics of the twenty-first century child.

Today's Child Is High Tech

Have you been in a child's bedroom recently? In a child's room you may find a cordless phone (perhaps with his own private line), sound system, television with access to cable or satellite programming, VCR, and computer with Internet access (which must include e-mail). A scanner and fax machine may be available as well. In the past, children wanted their own phone line. Now they all want their own private "on-line" Internet account. Even if your children do not have most of these gadgets, they are influenced by friends who do.

You will discover that today's child is high tech outside his bedroom as well. You might find that on his body he carries his own pager, cell phone, and mini-computer. Before this book is printed other technological advancements may be added, or some may replace the ones already mentioned here.

Why do we need to know the technological influences in a child's life? It is important to know how these advancements are affecting a child's communication skills, the way he thinks, the way he listens, and so forth.

Because today's children are living in such an instant information age, they tend to be more impatient and less focused, have shorter attention spans, and have weaker social and reading skills. It is becoming more difficult to capture their complete, undivided attention. My staff and I have noticed that children who attend summer camp go through a major withdrawal period as they adjust to being without a phone, radio, computer, television, e-mail, and video games.

Recently a heavy-hearted fifth-grade boy came to me to confess that a certain popular computer game had become so addictive that it began to control his life. Because of this addiction he and his mom had agreed that he would now be limited to playing this game "only one hour a day."

Today's child probably spends more time being on-line, playing video games, or sitting in front of a TV than he does talking with people. Therefore he may not have the listening skills he should have. He may look at you but not hear what you say. He may struggle with expressing himself or asking and answering questions. Be sensitive to this.

These same influences of technology are changing the adult world as well. As our world becomes more and more computerized, we may find ourselves spending less quality time with people. We may find it harder to relax and talk to people one-on-one. There are days that I have been talking to two people on the phone, plus one on-line, while two of my staff are in my office trying to meet with me. We are becoming accustomed to instant information, which enables us to work faster. But this has not made life easier or less stressful. Just the reverse, since we are doing more. This lifestyle can cause us to be impatient with others, especially children, who may not respond as instantly as we are accustomed to.

When we are discussing Christ with children we have to know

- what we want to say
- what the child needs to do
- how to keep the child's attention

We are dealing with children who are easily distracted and have short attention spans. They also bore easily and may have difficulty in expressing themselves verbally. We will lose their concentration if we can't connect with them or if we take too long trying.

Today's Child Is Overexposed

Children are confident living in the information age. Anything they want to know they can find. Not only can they locate information that they need; they can do so instantly. We are amazed at how technology has advanced our lives. *What will be the next advancement?* we wonder. However, children are being drowned with inappropriate material through the Internet, on television, and in movies. They have access to and the capability of viewing or downloading files that contain all types of harmful material.

We should be saddened at how fast children are losing their innocence. They are overexposed to many ugly elements in our society that rob them of their joy and purity. They are overexposed to sex and pornography. It is everywhere. This problem alone will have a long-lasting, devastating effect on their lives and the future of this country. Not only will it affect their marriages, families, and relationships, but it will also harm the way they think and what they value in people. Probably the greatest harm of all is how this will hinder their relationship with God. Sexual impurity becomes so addictive, and it places those who live this way in Satan's grip.

Children are also overexposed to violence, materialism, gambling, the Hollywood lifestyle, and inappropriate movies and television programs. Even sports have become too much of a negative influence. The messages presented by these and other harmful influences are in conflict with the message of God's plan for life. Kids today are confused about the true beauty and value of life that Christ offers. So many forces compete for their minds and hearts.

Parents, be aware of when, where, and how your child uses the Internet, e-mail, or chat rooms. Screen what your child views through television and movies. Pastors, provide training to the parents in your church so they will filter what comes into their homes and children's hearts.

Today's Child Is Desensitized

Children today are less sensitive to *human life*. Children today do not value human life as the children of previous generations did. Thanks to television, watching people die or be killed is a normal daily occurrence. Because of this, children's hearts are hardening. They see people as objects, not creations of God. This attitude can cause children to show little response to the sacrifice and pain of Christ's death. God still touches hearts when the gospel is discussed, and parents and teachers shouldn't be afraid of discussing it lest the kids ignore what they say. That story still has supernatural power, even with the most jaded and unchildlike youngsters. However, do not be surprised when children do not respond the way you think they should.

Children are also less sensitive to *spiritual things*. The number of "religious" choices has made any choice confusing. Just about any group can call itself "Christian." Society says to be tolerant of all groups and stresses that all groups are equal. This confuses children. Which group is telling the truth? Is truth important anyway? Not only are many of these messages confusing, but they can be disappointing as well. For instance, the continual public exposure of the lives of Christian leaders who have fallen or who lack integrity raises big questions about God in the minds of children.

Today's Child Is Nonrelational

Many children have no time for friendships and relationships, and they have no one to show them how to develop them. They no longer have time to simply "play." Many have forgotten how. This greatly affects how they interact with family, other children, teachers, and the church. They have difficulty sharing and knowing how to work out problems with others.

Children are looking for father and mother figures. They still respond to genuine encouragement and affection. They are hungry for a diet of discipline and love. As children face the divorces and busy schedules of their parents, the importance of Christian teachers, heroes, models, relatives, neighbors, and friends has risen. Today's children are searching for the true love that only Jesus can provide.

The ones they love the most may have hurt them, neglected them, abused them, or let them down. As a result, children are more skeptical. They are reluctant to get close to others for fear of being hurt again. But the beautiful thing about children is that they are so forgiving and accepting. It is easy to understand why Jesus loves children so much.

Today's Child Is Stressed

Children are involved in lots of activity. Many children of this generation are using daily planners in order to keep up with their schedule. They struggle to accomplish everything they have on their plate. Here are some examples of situations that add stress to today's child.

Today's child is stressed at home. Home stress has a variety of causes: tension between parents and/or with siblings; lack of sleep; a poor diet; little time to play or relax; the feeling that the child cannot talk to his parents; negative music; too much television or too many video games; staying secluded in his room away from family; and lack of discipline.

Today's child is stressed at school. The average child faces pressure from mounting homework; fear of bullies or harmful activities; hurrying from class to class; too many extracurricular activities (or not enough time for extracurricular activity); peer pressure; negative language; and sometimes heavy competition (for grades, scholarships, positions on a team, etc.).

Today's child is stressed at church. He may struggle to understand the terminology. He doesn't know what to do with sermons or lessons that he cannot apply to his daily life. He attends boring Bible classes and church services that do not involve his senses or learning style and that give lots of information, but not enough answers. And he is unlikely to find one thing he really needs at church: mentors, relationships, and individuals he can trust.

Note: Children's activities must be fun. Bible classes should include games, music, hands-on activities, and worship. They should also involve occasional high-energy events (rallies, goals, competition, special guests, etc.). Two of the greatest teaching tools are games and songs. Lecturing *about* God does not meet the needs of today's child. He needs to be shown how to have a relationship *with* God and not just hear facts about the Bible. A child's Bible classroom should be a fun, calm, and active learning environment.

How do we reach the child who is stressed? We help him relax. We involve his senses. We build relationships. We create a fun environment. We include physical activities that allow him to release energy. We read to him. We talk about things that interest him. We see what else is on his mind. We tell him and show him that God loves him. We use music. Music is such a powerful influence on a child's attitude. You can use music when a child wakes up, comes home from school, visits your office, enters your classroom, or prepares for bed. Music has the power to add stress or relieve stress. Children also need a place and time for quiet. So do adults.

Today's Child Is Afraid

He is afraid of death, of what happens after death, of how he will die. (Will he be killed violently or in an accident, or will he die of some dread disease?) He fears bullies and is continually afraid of not being accepted by peers, of being considered stupid or cowardly or otherwise deficient. He may fear his teachers, the government, or other authority figures.

He is afraid of the future: afraid he might not be able to buy a car, go to college, or get a job. Nuclear-holocaust scares of earlier generations have been replaced with environmental-disaster scenarios today. Environmental activists have written books for children and provided classroom material for teachers, making many of today's children into fearful environmental crusaders.

Too many children feel unable to trust anyone, and they live with the nagging sense that their parents will divorce. They are afraid of failure, and some are even afraid to do their best because it may not be good enough or may go unnoticed.

Children are afraid that God cannot or will not do anything to help them. But today's child is *not* afraid of God. Today's society does not fear God. Our families and churches do not fear God.

Scripture has the power to calm our fears. Use Scripture to reassure children of God's purpose, position, protection, and power. Show them that God knows them, loves them, cares for them, and is strong enough to protect them.

Today's Child Is Angry

He may be angry at adults who seem to have failed him or neglected him, whether teachers, parents, or leaders at church. He is likely to be angry at classmates, siblings, or friends who have hurt him or let him down. Although he is not likely to admit it, he may very well be angry at God.

Several aspects of his life fuel such anger: physical or emotional abuse from the violent adults around him, violent and angry music, cynical TV shows, the violence of TV news, and his own sense of helplessness, loneliness, and lack of protection.

How do we help children deal with anger? First, a child should learn how to talk it out. He should be encouraged that it is safe for him to talk with those who care about him (parents, siblings, friends, teachers). He should learn the value of exercise. Then rather than going and hitting his pillow, he will find release in going outside to play. He should be encouraged to pray and let God comfort him. He should be taught Scriptures that give him comfort and power. And finally he should see the positive example of how his parents and other respected adults deal with their own anger.

Today's Child Is Depressed

The eyes of today's children have a sadder look than in years past. They show high levels of frustration and hopelessness. They have questions. They have hurts. They do not know how to properly express their emotions. They feel alone and do not have someone to talk to about their problems. Nor do they have the time. Many do not have friends.

More children than ever are under the care of professional counselors. Among today's children there is a greater use of and dependency on behavior-changing medication.

Today's Child Is Very, Very Special to God

This book is addressing ways that we can better understand children and therefore better lead them to Christ. But as you analyze the children you know and improve your methods of discussing your faith in Christ with them, remember this: Children are precious in His sight. Someone once said, "A man is tallest when he stoops to help a child." Do not forget how important children are to the heavenly Father.

Today's Child Needs the Lord (and He Doesn't Know It)

The Good News is still good, and it is still news. It is the best kept secret on earth. We cannot assume that because a child attends church or lives in a Christian family he realizes his need for Christ. We must tell him about his need and the way it has been met. What children do you know who need to hear about the Lord? Will you make time to talk about Christ with them?

HELPING TODAY'S CHILD

In addition to the suggestions mentioned above, other areas of a child's life should be included in the pursuit to better understand him. Gathering information from the following areas of your child's life will provide you with a better picture of him.

1. Temperament. Is he sanguine, melancholy, choleric, or phlegmatic? Knowing this will tell you how best to relate to him. For more information, see Beverly LaHaye, *How to Develop Your Child's Temperament* (Eugene, Oreg.: Harvest House, 1999).

2. Birth order. A child's "birthplace" in the family usually af-

fects the way he responds to life. I recommend you read Kevin Lehman's *The New Birth Order Book* (Grand Rapids: Revell, 1998).

3. Learning style(s). Most of us are either auditory, visual, or kinesthetic learners, or a mixture of a couple of these. Cynthia Tobias explores learning styles in *The Way They Learn* (Colorado Springs: Focus on the Family, 1998).

4. Medical history. Does he struggle with allergies or asthma? What is your family's medical history? When a child is battling an illness of some type it may hinder his ability to learn, listen, etc.

5. Family. Do you have a happy home? a Christian home? Does the child get along well with his siblings, and does he feel accepted and loved by you?

The better you understand a child the more equipped you will be to meet his physical, educational, emotional, and spiritual needs. One thing always happens when you better understand a child . . . you grow to love him more.

Chapter Four
Understanding the Faith of a Child

When you are saved, the old life has passed away. You have begun a new life. The Bible says you become a new creation, a new creature. You may have been taught that if you do not know the exact date, time, and place of your salvation, then you probably are not saved. Although it is a positive thing to know your spiritual birth date, it is not a requirement. The important thing is that you have, by faith, accepted Christ's death for you.

Being able to recall the time and place of one's conversion to Christianity is an added security for children (and for adults as well). Salvation is a life-changing experience. We should visit that memory often. We should also discuss that experience with others whenever we get the opportunity to do so. We should look back to see how God has changed us and see how He is still changing us. We should never take for granted the value of Christ's death and resurrection for us.

Parents want to help their children avoid as many of the struggles, doubts, and uncertainties that surround salvation as possible. They want their children to be certain of their decision to become Christians. The good news is that children can be certain, but they will not be unless we help them. The Bible says in Proverbs 29:15 that "a child left to itself disgraces his mother." This means that a child who is not taught or disciplined in the ways of the Lord will fail at life and embarrass his family. He will fail if he is left to mature alone. The opposite of this principle is that a child who is taught and disciplined in the ways of the Lord will be strong and equipped for life. He will not be as confused, weak, or vulnerable to Satan's attacks as he would be otherwise.

A large percentage of Christians struggle with knowing when they actually became Christians. They do not remember the date. They don't remember many details. They are not sure if they were old enough or knew what they were doing. This can cause years of doubt and frustration. If Satan cannot keep a person from becoming a Christian, then he will try to defeat him by causing him to doubt his salvation. This is why we want to give children the time they need to grow, understand, and undergo a complete conversion experience. We want them to do it right the first time so they will not have to worry about it later.

After talking with thousands of parents who have brought their children to my office, I can sadly say that many parents are unsure about their own salvation experience. They are not sure when it happened, and they admit that the uncertainty has bothered them for many years. This may describe you. If it does, that can influence how you teach your own children about Christ. Hopefully, you will want to help your child have a solid conversion experience that develops into a strong and growing relationship with Christ.

SALVATION IS A BIRTH EXPERIENCE

The Bible tells us that *becoming a Christian is a birth experience.* A human life begins with the union of two cells and then a nine-month pregnancy before the birth actually occurs. After the birth, special care must be given to the new baby until he or she can take care of himself or herself. We cannot remember our physical births. We must rely on our parents' stories and photos for the details. It is obvious that we have been born, but we are dependent on others to tell us how it happened.

Salvation has many similar characteristics to physical birth, as you will see in a moment, but it also has differences. It is so important that a child has someone to help him come to know the Lord. It is also important to have someone who can help him recall the events leading to his salvation and the growth events that have occurred since. But a child must make his own decision, know what he decided, and remember the decision.

If a child cannot remember the event, there may not be an event to remember. If he cannot point to a single event, he may be able to describe a series of events that led to his salvation. When a child is unsure about when and where he accepted Christ but knows that he is a Christian, help him take a look back and review the events and changes that have taken place in his life. Every Christian should be able to give an account of how he came to faith in Christ, even if it is not crystal clear. Helping a child verbalize his testimony is such a great help in establishing a landmark that he can refer to all his life. If he relies on his parents' memory of the event, he may struggle later in life with its validity.

Spiritual birth and physical birth have a lot in common. Take a look at the following five categories, the different possibilities that can happen when birth is near.

Full-term Birth

This birth is the result of a full-term pregnancy. The baby is born after nine months of life and growth inside the womb. During these nine months the parents-to-be prepare for the new arrival. The mother attends doctor's appointments to monitor the health of herself and the baby. She has exercises to do. She must have a healthy diet. The parents choose possible names. They buy what they will need (clothes, furniture, supplies). The parents know the baby is coming, so they prepare the best they can. They want the birth to be the best it can be. They want their new child to have the best life they can give him or her.

Usually, prior to the birth, the parents go to birthing classes. This is where they learn what to expect from the time labor begins, through the delivery process. During the class couples practice procedures that are intended to help the delivery go smoothly. Relaxing, breathing, and focusing activities are demonstrated and rehearsed.

The full-term birth is the model for a child's spiritual birth. We want a child's conversion to be the result of a *full term* of preparation. We want a child to be ready when God begins to speak to him. We want the child to experience a healthy birth. The child should be given plenty of time to develop. Sometimes it seems that a child's spiritual birth will never come. But we do not rush it, though we may need to induce labor if the child needs some encouragement. A child may need a nudge, but not a shove. Also, we need to be able to recognize the difference between *real labor* and *false labor*. False labor would be when a child is just asking normal, inquisitive questions. Real labor would be when a child asks questions that demonstrate a deep conviction, willingness, and understanding of the commitment to receive Christ.

Healthy babies need prenatal care, and so do healthy Christians. Children need us to teach, listen, model, and evaluate them. The growth prior to birth is almost as important as the birth (decision) itself. A child can be born without prenatal care, but the chances are that he will not be as healthy as babies who do receive it. Not every child has the blessing of having parents who will provide him with the spiritual environment that he needs. But God wants us to prepare the way for children to be born again. He wants us to be equipped and involved in leading our children to become Christians.

A fourth-grade Sunday school teacher I know tries to spend a few minutes each Sunday with one of the children in his class. He spends these moments getting to know each child. He strives to learn where each child stands spiritually. He has led many children to the Lord in this way. Many times children understand what it means to become a Christian, but other times they do not. In either case, a personal one-on-one time is what helps them complete their decision. Leading children to Christ is all about building relationships with them.

Premature Birth

Some babies come early. When this happens a higher risk is involved because of the possibility that vital organs have not fully developed. Though we live in a day of great advancements in medicine and technology, preemie babies are not treated like full-term babies. They require extra care and constant monitoring.

My sister's first child, Christina, was born early. Instead of taking that precious little girl home, Bill and Sheri had to leave her in the hospital incubator a little longer. When they did finally get to take her home they took a monitor with her. For the first few weeks she was under careful observation. Her parents and the doctors wanted to make sure that she was going to be strong enough on her own. Only when she got stronger was the monitor finally removed.

Most preschoolers have questions about God. They also have great affection for God. When parents encourage their preschoolers to accept Christ they run the risk of creating a spiritual preemie. A child could possibly be saved that young, but most children are not spiritually capable. When the preschool child begins to show an interest in the Lord, we should feed that interest. We don't suggest to the child that he should immediately become a Christian. He is too small and weak. He needs time in the womb first. He may act or sound like he is ready, but we know that in most cases he has not fully developed on the inside. God can save a two-year-old if He wants to do so, but we know that this usually is not the way He works.

Early in my ministry I thought that if a child was old enough to want to pray the sinner's prayer then he was qualified to become a full-fledged Christian. Now I know that this is not true. When young children begin to pray and seek to become Christians, it is usually the spiritual pregnancy that is taking place, not the birth itself. The section on the four stages of spiritual development later in this chapter will address this more. Children are individuals, and some preschoolers are ready for salvation—but that is an exception.

Emergency Birth

One of our church members delivered his wife's baby in our church parking lot. The baby came before they could get to the birthing center. Our church was the closest exit, so they stopped and the baby was born in their van. Each birth experience is unique. Some are easy; some happen quickly. Others can take many hours or even develop complications.

Both of our boys were born after long hours of labor. On each occasion we got to the hospital and watched several movies before our son decided to come into the world. When Patrick, our second son, was born, the doctor came really close to performing a Caesarian section. Patrick had managed to get wrapped up in the umbilical cord, so it was kind of touchy to say the least. I got on the phone and called my mom to start praying. She prayed, and Patrick unwound himself so the birth could take place without surgery. In each of these cases time—and prayer—became a major factor.

Sometimes we don't have the extra time we would like to spend teaching, nurturing, or modeling the Christian life to children. Noncustodial parents who have experienced divorce don't get the same amount of time as custodial parents do. Grandparents who see their grandchildren only a few days a year have limited influence. A youth group hosting a children's Bible club on a mission trip might have just one opportunity to present the gospel of Christ. Christian families on vacation sometimes have opportunities to talk with other families about their faith. None of these examples offers much time to build relationships, but God will bless these opportunities if we let Him.

One of the teachers in our children's ministry walks every morning for exercise. During her walk she takes time to say hello to children who are near her house waiting to catch the bus. She has seen this as her opportunity to present Christ in her neighborhood. And God has blessed it. Several of these children come from rough, sad home situations. But they have responded to her love and her witness. She talks to them about God. She tells them Bible stories. She gives them Scriptures to memorize. She encourages them to make good choices in their lives though they are surrounded by wickedness.

Recently, she realized that one of the families was moving away. Feeling the Holy Spirit move her, she presented Christ's claims to a brother and a sister, and both accepted Christ. She saw the urgency and took advantage of the opportunity.

One summer our church sponsored children's Bible clubs all over the city. The response was great. One little boy, Kelvin, attended every day. He attended the club that Lois Ann, my wife, led. He came early, was the last to leave, and became our son Ben's twin that week. They had a blast together. At the close of each day they had big smiles, Kool-Aid lips, and bodies dripping with sweat. On the last day we found Kelvin's name tag. It had torn away from the string around his neck and was lying on the ground. He was so active, that name tag just could not survive. Those were sweet memories.

A week or two after the club ended I received a call from one of our members from that neighborhood. While crossing the street in his neighborhood, Kelvin was hit by a car and killed. I was the only white man at his funeral. I could tell that many of those who attended wondered who I was. I will never forget his little body in that casket. His lifeless body lay clutching a pair of drumsticks. I was glad to know that Lois Ann and her team of volunteers made an impact on his life for Jesus in the five days they were together.

God will use what time you have available to teach children. In what may seem to be an "emergency" situation, when witnessing seems to be more urgent, God has a plan. Even though you may get just one brief opportunity, His Word and your witness can go a long way. Use opportunities you have to witness to the children you influence. You may not know until you get to heaven the impact that you had.

Stillborn Birth

To our shock and sadness some babies are miscarried or stillborn. When the time of birth comes there is no life. There are no baby cries, no good news, no tears of joy. The body is limp. The child is not breathing or moving. The baby is dead. Usually, the obstetrician will discover this before the birth occurs, but sometimes it will come as a shock to the parents and physicians. In either case it is a painfully sad tragedy.

My sister Sheri had twins who lived only one day before they went to heaven. What a sorrowful time this was for all of us. Maybe you or someone close to you has had a similar experience.

I compare these examples to the child who joins the church or gets baptized without truly being born again. He or she goes through the motions of spiritual birth, but there is no sign of new life. Our world doesn't need more church members; it needs more Christians. As we better understand how children develop spiritually we are able to identify the characteristics of a live birth. We take every precaution we can to ensure a healthy birth.

Aborted Birth

Abortion occurs because of inconvenience, peer pressure, ignorance, or all of these. The baby is viewed as an inconvenience to the parent, someone puts pressure on the mother to dispose of the child, or the fatal decision is made out of ignorance (or incorrect information). The same thing happens spiritually to a child when parents, teachers, or pastors squelch a child's spirit by responding harshly or inappropriately.

Our fast-paced lifestyle tempts us to rush through life's most precious moments. Many of these moments involve our children. Don't be too busy for your child's spiritual life.

If we make hasty decisions based on convenience, what others think, tradition, and/or lack of information, then we may be guilty of spiritually aborting a child's faith.

Leading children to Christ is not always convenient. Discussions about Christ don't always happen the way we plan or when we are ready for them. Furthermore, leading a child to Christ should not be based on what other parents are doing. Observe what other parents and teachers do, but be wise. How the majority of people approach the faith of a child may not be appropriate for you and your child.

Physicians should take every reasonable precaution to avoid malpractice. Their first commitment is to their patient, not to the public. The same is true for those who assist in the spiritual birth and health of a child.

Note: Please read this next section very carefully. It will be one of the lessons you remember most about this book. It will become one of the greatest tools you use in understanding where your child is spiritually. Discovering the stages of a child's faith took my ministry to children, parents, and children's leaders to a deeper level. It has become one of the most eye-opening, pivotal experiences in my ministry. I did not discover these stages in child psychology or childhood education courses in seminary or graduate school. I became aware of these through observing and personally talking with thousands of boys and girls about their faith.

THE FOUR STAGES OF FAITH DEVELOPMENT

Young Timothy's faith grew as the result of the faithful teaching of his mother and grandmother (2 Timothy 3:15). As his faith matured he grew into a wise young man. Timothy is an example of how the faithful, godly example of a parent (and grandparent) can impact a child's life. His childhood also illustrates how different elements such as knowledge, wisdom, and faith work together to build a strong Christian life. A child's faith is strong, oftentimes stronger than that of adults. But that faith needs to grow. Once a child begins to show signs of faith in God we should begin to feed his faith.

Understanding a child's level of faith is one step in helping his faith grow. Discovering the four stages of a child's faith was revolutionary for me. It changed how I see children. Understanding how a child's faith develops helps us to be more sensitive to what he needs from us. But adults are quick to label children. It is usually a mistake when we do. We should not label or put children in categories in order to limit their abilities. When we categorize children it should be so that we may understand them better. As a child matures, the way he thinks changes. His ability to understand also changes. We want to be able to communicate to children in language that they can understand.

Do not be surprised if a child has one foot in one stage and the other foot in the next stage. Most children are in transition. My prayer is that these categories will help you better understand and identify your child's spiritual needs.

The Discovering Stage
Age: birth to five years
Key Terms: first impressions, positive feelings,
  foundation building, sensory motor experiences
Our Role: cultivator (preparing the soil for seeds
  that will be planted later)

This stage is best described as "the process of storing new information." During this first stage of life, a child stores huge amounts of information every day. Preschoolers are naturally inquisitive. They are born with a desire to discover the world around them. It is so much fun to watch them play and try to figure out life. During this time their brains constantly ask the question, "What is that?"

Children at this stage discover and store information through the use of their *senses* and their *emotions.* Their eyes, ears, taste buds, and hands are constantly downloading information into their minds. This is how they formulate their first impressions of life, which will influence their later impressions about God. It is so important that we provide children at this stage with good impressions.

Impressions about God are being made through playtime, mealtime, bedtime, stories, songs, hugs, games, Sunday school classes, nature walks, and so forth. A child's impression of God is directly related to his relationship with you and the happy (or sad) feelings he gets when he is around you. If he loves being around you, then he will love the learning environment you provide. Parents, siblings, relatives, teachers, and playmates all affect a child during this stage of discovery.

Deuteronomy 6:7 tells us to teach our children as we "walk along the road." This best describes the teaching method that is most effective with this age child. It is the daily lessons of life's experiences (planned and unplanned) that mean the most. Preschoolers do not sit still very long unless it is to hear a good story, look at a book, pet a cuddly animal, or eat something that they like. Their attention span is not long. But, thankfully, they do respond to their feelings and touch, sight, sound, and taste . . . life's senses.

Parents should provide preschoolers as many opportunities as they can each day to use their senses. They should also look for and take advantage of all the spontaneous teaching opportunities that come throughout the day. We do not want to wait until a child can understand what it means to become a Christian before we begin teaching him. The discovery stage is when we begin to prepare the soil for the seeds that will be planted later.

Most children this age cannot fully understand what it means to be a Christian. However, this is when the *foundation* begins. Do not make the mistake of thinking that children at this stage cannot learn. Just the opposite. They learn constantly. More importantly, their adult attitude and personality are being formed during this time, which affects everything else they will learn, do, and become. Reading to your preschooler about God, creation, families, stories about Jesus, people of the Bible (including some stories about children), and so forth is a valuable way to help build a strong spiritual foundation. Undoubtedly, it will be the nursery workers who faithfully (and oftentimes thanklessly) teach preschoolers about God who get the greatest rewards in heaven. Help your preschooler discover the things of God. Do not leave it up to someone else.

Provide the child with daily experiences that involve seeing, hearing, and touching. Use these experiences to introduce him to God. Teach him the characteristics of God. Help him know that God is a real person and is personal. God cares about him. God made him, knows everything about him, and, most of all, loves him. Teach the child about creation, the importance of the Bible, God's design for the family, who Jesus is, and that Jesus came to earth to tell us that God loves us. Review by asking questions. Be ready for and encourage discussion. Accept all questions that your child might have. Be careful not to start with stories that are too harsh or scary (e.g., David and Bathsheba, the crucifixion of Jesus, the book of Revelation, etc.). Daily Bible stories are valuable during this formative stage. Bible storybooks, books for preschoolers, songs, nature activities, art activities, and anything that is hands-on are a plus. Memorizing songs and Scriptures should be fun, not a chore.

The Discerning Stage
Age: four to eight years
Key Terms: gathering facts, exploring the Bible,
    curiosity, asking questions
Our Role: planter (planting seeds through
    teaching, modeling, observing, answering)

This stage is best described as a time of questioning. During the first part of the discovering stage children just accept what they experience as a part of life without really thinking much about it. They usually don't begin to ask deep questions until later. But as they leave that stage they begin to ask questions like "Why did God do that?" or "How did God do that?" They may ask their questions outwardly, or they may ask them internally. That will greatly depend on their personality and the relationship or openness they have with the ones around them.

"Who created God?" "How did God always exist?" "What happens when we die?" "Will there be animals in heaven?" "What is a Christian?" "Mommy, am I a Christian?" "Can I be a Christian?" "Where is heaven?" "What is hell?" "Why is everyone eating crackers and grape juice?" "Can I have some?" "Will I get baptized one day?" "When can I get baptized?" "Why are those people who are talking to the pastor crying?" Have you ever been asked questions such as these?

Adults are often uncomfortable during this stage because the questions children ask can be hard to answer. They can also come at inconvenient times. Sometimes questions at this stage can be nonstop, wear on our nerves, and/or be asked when we least expect them. Wise adults will take advantage of the teaching opportunities that this stage presents. Questions may come during quiet observations at church, at bedtime when you are trying to get your child to go to sleep, in traffic, or at the unlikeliest moment. Please don't ignore any question, whether it seems small or great.

The Deciding Stage
Age: seven to twelve years
Key Terms: conviction, struggle, faith,
    transformation
Our Role: caretaker (providing food for the new
    plant that it may grow)

During this stage of faith development a child asks himself "How does this *affect me?*" "Does what the pastor (or teacher or parent) said today apply to me?" "How did he know what I was thinking?" "Do I need to make a decision with my life concerning Christ?" "Am I going to follow Christ with my life?" "Should I do it now or wait?" "What will others think if I do?" "Do I have to make my decision public?" "If I decide to become a Christian, do I have to get baptized?" "My friend (or relative) got baptized. Should I get baptized?"

The child begins to sort through all of the information he has and realizes that he has to make a decision. It is not enough just to know these things; he must make one of the following decisions: He can either reject Jesus, or he can make a personal commitment with his own life to Jesus.

Often before someone makes the decision to give his life to Christ a battle takes place. Children at this stage may begin to have a personal unrest or struggle of some type. This may be demonstrated through behavior, attitude, performance, attention span, emotions, or in other ways. However, he may not show any obvious signs that a struggle exists. Encourage the child at this stage to trust God. Let him know that you are there to help him too. Encourage him to go ahead with his decision, not to put it off, and not to be afraid.

Younger children who want to become Christians before they understand what they are doing do not struggle at all. They don't put as much thought into it. The adults they admire have told them that this is what they need to do, and they just do it. They don't question or count the cost. It is normal for children who were raised in a Christian environment to want to be Christians. It is all they know, and everyone they are close to is already a Christian. They feel left out of the family when they realize that they are not Christians like everyone else.

During the deciding stage it is obvious that the child has moved from being curious to being convicted. He has chosen to have personal faith instead of depending on the faith of his parents or others. He now has a passion to please Christ instead of mere pleasantness from knowing what it means to be a Christian.

The Discipling Stage
Age: ten years and up
Key Terms: establishing habits, consistency,
     maturity, growing deeper, doctrine
Our Role: pruner (shaping, encouraging, the
     growing plant)

Discipleship should begin well before a child gives his life to Jesus. Ideally you should begin discipling a child when he or she is just a preschooler. But once a child becomes a born-again believer you must take discipleship very seriously. This is when many of his spiritual habits for life will be formed. The Christian life does not stop once a child makes the decision to become a Christian. That is just the beginning. The next steps are obedience, growth, maturity, and consistency. But most children will not experience these steps of discipleship unless we follow up with them.

Many discipleship activities are helpful when a child is young. Memorizing Bible verses, daily Bible reading, daily prayer, witnessing to others, inviting friends to church, giving tithes and offerings, and acts of kindness are healthy favorites. These habits can be established even before your child becomes a Christian. They can be tools that God will use to help your child become a Christian as well as help him or her grow after he or she has taken that step of faith.

One important thing to remember is that you cannot teach a child to live the Christian life if you are not living it too. You cannot take the approach of "Do what I say, not what I do." Instead, you must live a life that says, "Do what I say *and* what I do." You should live a life that causes a child to say, "I want to be like that when I am grown." What an impact you can make on your child.

When a child becomes a preteen (somewhere around the age of ten), discipleship is no longer optional. You must help him establish lifelong habits that will strengthen, encourage, teach, mature, prepare, and protect him. Not only do you want to keep a daily check on your child's discipleship activities, but you should also meet at least once each week to talk about the week. Talk about the challenges, the progress, the blessings, the failures, the lessons learned, the questions he has, and his accomplishments. Make it a parent/child bonding time.

Discipleship should not be a rigid time full of criticism. It is a time to build up a child and establish a positive relationship. It is a time of open discussion as well as discussion of selected topics you prepare prior to the meeting. It is a time to evaluate the successes and failures, but more importantly, it is a time to show the child the power, truth, joy, and faithfulness of God.

Parents who do not start early sitting down with their children on a regular basis to talk will find it more difficult, if not impossible, to communicate about bigger issues at later times (sex, peer pressure, problems, decisions, finances, dating).

Children are discipled by our examples. Our outlook on life shapes theirs. Our relationship with God influences their relationship with God. But more important, our relationships with each other are what they observe the most. Remember, Christianity is built on a relationship. One of the greatest gifts you can give your children is the gift of good relationships. How you treat your spouse, parents, siblings, children, neighbors, and pastor teaches them more than telling them about God. We show them God by the way we live, react, decide, respond, talk, and listen.

Children are discipled by our instruction. Discipleship should include a time to study Scripture, discuss it, set goals, confess sin, discuss victories, and pray. You may want to meet with one child individually or gather a small group of children together for this reason.

Parents, teachers, pastors, do you know your children well? Think about these four stages of faith. Where are your children spiritually? Can you determine the spiritual stage that they are facing?

HOW TO PREPARE CHILDREN

How do these four stages affect the way parents and teachers approach children about God's plan for salvation?

1. Parents and teachers should start early teaching their children about God. Spiritual training should begin before a child is two years old.

2. Parents and teachers should not wait until their children seek to know about God.

3. Parents and teachers should be positive and encouraging when their children express the desire to accept Christ.

4. Parents and teachers should not mistake a child's curiosity with his conviction. Sometimes new parents will mistake false labor for real labor.

5. There will usually be some sort of "kick in the womb" long before labor begins.

6. Parents and teachers should not abandon a child as he begins making his decision to become a Christian. His decision is not completely up to him. He needs our wisdom, encouragement, evaluation, and direction.

7. Parents and teachers should not cease guiding a child once he decides to accept Christ.

8. Parents and teachers should give a child's decision some time to bear fruit. They should watch to see if he begins to show signs of a conversion experience.

9. Parents and teachers should pray earnestly for their children.

10. Parents and teachers should pray for themselves, asking the Holy Spirit to lead them and give them wisdom.

ENSURING PROPER PREPARATION

At a national conference of pastors and church leaders years ago, 89 percent of the attendees felt that children were joining their churches unsaved. Most were frustrated because they didn't know what they could do about it. No pastor wants to turn away a child or hurt a parent who is sincere about his or her child's decision. This is a special time in a family's life, and we must wisely and tenderly help families know what to do. Realizing that children are not little adults, churches have begun to develop different methods for handling children. Our job as pastors, parents, and children's ministry leaders is to build a bridge between childhood and adulthood and hold each child's hand until he has crossed the bridge.

A large percentage of people are saved between the ages of eight and twelve. For example, according to the Home Mission Board of the Southern Baptist Convention, in 1994 Southern Baptists baptized 378,463 people. Of that number notice the percentages according to age:

5 and under — 1%
6–11 — 30.9%
(6–8 — 12.2%, 9–11 — 18.7%)
12–17 — 23.5%
18 and up — 44.6%

Based on my personal experience with thousands of children and parents, I have noticed that for some reason most children under the age of seven and a half are not spiritually mature enough to make the commitment to become a Christian. Children at this age may be a lot more curious than they are convicted. A large percent of those who make a decision under the age of seven and a half tend to have doubts about the decision they made as a child and strongly consider making another decision later in their middle to late teens (if they are brave enough to do it again) because:

1. They don't remember much about the first experience. They base it too much on what their parents remember.

2. They were not mature enough to see the whole picture. Because they are concrete thinkers they are attracted to what they can see (e.g., baptism, the Lord's Supper). They may have difficulty with God because they cannot see, hear, or touch Him. They cannot think abstractly.

3. They tend to have more doubts and need more assurance than those who are older. Satan loves when this happens. It is one of his most powerful tools used to defeat Christians. He is the author of confusion.

4. There seems to be a lack of completion. Usually a child in this case will know all the facts about becoming a Christian, but he may not understand them completely or feel a conviction to repent of sin. He may base his decision to follow Christ on his knowledge instead of his brokenness.

These problems could be avoided in most cases if enough individual time is given to the child to help him understand and grow. In some cases a young child can still understand enough to be converted if it's not a rushed decision, but in most cases a young child needs more time to grow. From the time he expresses an initial interest in becoming a Christian he may need more time to understand what it means, experience conviction, etc. God will do the rest. Too much emphasis is put on "the sinner's prayer" or baptism and not enough emphasis put on teaching, discipleship, or growth.

I've known parents of children as young as twenty-two months to lead their child to pray "the prayer" to ask Jesus into their hearts. I'm not questioning God. He can save children who are still in the womb if He wants to. I am questioning parental and church responsibility. We must do a better job raising our children to know and love God. Any child can be led to pray the sinner's prayer. But as you will discover later, there are at least six signs that a child is ready to accept Christ as his Lord. Prayer is a definite part of the commitment to follow Christ, but not the only part.

Have you ever heard children learn the pledge to the American flag? It can be hilarious. Many times they mispronounce words, get them in the wrong order, or even substitute more familiar words in place of ones they do not know (e.g., "invisible" in place of "indivisible"). But most children, once they have learned the pledge, do not immediately know what it means. Chances are, they know it is a way to honor our country, but they do not know what the words mean. Words like "allegiance," "republic," and "indivisible" have little meaning to children. As a matter of fact, most adults do not know the full meaning of those words either. They have been taught to say the pledge but not to understand it. Like learning the pledge, children often learn to pray to ask Jesus into their hearts without knowing what it means.

So many times parents are caught off guard when their children come to them with the news that they want to "ask Jesus into their hearts" (or that they have already done so). Most parents have not been involved enough in the process and consequently are puzzled as to what to do with the child's request.

Sometimes adults feel that if the child's first decision to receive Christ as Savior isn't real, then God will take care of it later when the child *is* ready. We know that to be true in many cases, but if we know how to help at this impressionable time, we should do so. We know God wants us to be involved in the process. He has stated that clearly (Deuteronomy 6:4–7; Ephesians 6:4).

One more point needs to be addressed. When a person feels the need to make a second decision for Christ it is usually a lot more difficult to make it public the second time. Satan tries to make that person feel embarrassed or appear to be confused.

We have observed the importance that a child's age plays in his readiness for salvation. We have listed specific traits that help us better understand how children grow in their faith. However, *this does not mean that a child younger than eight years old cannot be born again. Neither does it mean that every child once he turns eight years old is ready to become a Christian.* A child's spiritual birth date is up to God and not us. But God has given us the task of helping Him in the child's preparation. Prepare the soil, sow, water, and then harvest.

Children ask questions about lots of subjects because they are naturally curious. When it comes to salvation, *do not mistake a child's normal curiosity for conviction.* They are distinctly different and both important, used by God at different stages.

The faith of a child is a great thing. Nothing is more precious than the faith of a child. Jesus used it as an illustration to rebuke adults. But most preschool children (birth to six years) don't know the difference between fantasy and faith. They will believe anything without stopping to think about its reality or consequences. They don't even question it if we say it is so. It never crosses their minds not to believe in Jesus. This is the best time to influence a child about God.

The impact made during this stage plays an important part

in their future decision to become Christians. As they leave this stage we have the chance to teach them the truth, as what is pretend begins to vanish. It is important that they not only know but also understand the truth so they can make their very own personal commitment to Jesus. The desire of young children to become Christians is usually linked more to the love for their parents and teachers than to Jesus. Our relationships with children should be a stepping-stone to their relationship with God.

Chapter Five

How to Know if a Child Is Ready to Become a Christian

How will I know when my child is ready to receive Christ? This question grips the hearts of Christian parents of young children. There is great value in understanding how children mature spiritually. Let's take a close-up view of the child who is ready to accept Christ.

WHAT ARE SOME SIGNS THAT A CHILD IS READY TO ACCEPT CHRIST?

Does Salvation Make Sense?

Does the child really understand what it means to become a Christian? Children can memorize and repeat what they have heard their parents and teachers say, but that doesn't mean that they understand it all. Neither does it mean that they are personally committed to those truths.

A few questions can determine where a child is spiritually.

- Can the child explain in his or her own words the basics of becoming a Christian? When explaining how one becomes a Christian, does the child use "good works" answers such as "going to church, reading the Bible, getting baptized, praying, being good," etc.? Or do his answers mention his need for forgiveness?

- Does the child have an affection for Jesus or a strong desire to be close to Him? Does he show a passion to follow Jesus or just a basic knowledge of the facts about Him?

- Does he distinguish between salvation and baptism? It is normal for young children to identify the act of baptism as the actual salvation experience.

The point here is that we should not allow children to enter into the Christian life ignorantly. Ignorance and faith are distinctly different. No one needs a doctor's degree in systematic theology to enter the kingdom of God, but he does have to understand what salvation means.

Please do not wait until a child can provide *all* the right answers before you begin to take him seriously. He may not have all the detailed information he needs in order to fully explain salvation (many adults struggle trying to put such an awesome experience into words), but he may have a heart that is very ready to trust Christ.

Children depend on us to teach them about God's gift of salvation. Once we have planted God's Word into their hearts and minds, we must begin to water those spiritual seeds until the young plants are strong enough to stand on their own. Part of the joy of leading children to Christ is helping and watching them grow and begin to personally embrace Christ. But do not confuse a child's ability to use "church words" with having a true understanding. Many times parents consider their children's questions (or correct answers) to be the entrance exam for salvation. Understanding the basic terms about salvation does not mean a child has experienced it.

Parents want to make sure that their child experiences more than just learning what it means to become a Christian. It is very important that a child *understands* what it means. If a child understands, then his commitment to accept Christ will be stronger, more genuine.

When I talk to children about accepting Christ, I stop several times throughout the conversation and ask, "Does what I have been talking about make sense?" If something doesn't make sense, I will ask him to tell me what it is so we can talk about it. If he is still unclear or unsure about what to do, I don't push him. The Holy Spirit has not finished preparing him.

One Sunday morning, Kendra, who was almost nine years old, was riding with me in one of the church golf carts. We were picking up people and transporting them from the parking lot to the worship center. We had been talking about what a beautiful day it was when out of the blue she looked up at me and said, "I love God." That blew me away. She was so serious. She then went on to explain, "That is why I became a Christian. I already loved God, so I thought, *I might as well become a Christian.*" It was as if she woke up one day and realized that loving God was not enough. She realized that there was another step . . . accepting Him and committing her life to Him. Becoming a Christian finally made sense.

Does the Child Exhibit a Brokenness over Sin?

Does the child demonstrate a personal need or desire to repent of his sin? Is the child ashamed of the sin in his life? Knowing what sin is is not the same as being ashamed of sin. If a child is not repentant but goes ahead and makes a decision to become a Christian, then his decision is premature and incomplete. Letting a child think that he can become a Christian without repentance gives him false assurance. As a result, he may never repent and therefore never completely finish becoming a Christian.

Loving Jesus is an important part of becoming a Christian, but that is not enough. If a child is led to think that he can be a Christian without repentance, he does not fully understand the need for a Savior. He may love Jesus but not feel the need for Him in his life. He may live his life thinking that everything is OK when it is not.

Becoming a Christian is not "figuring out what everything means." It is humbly coming before God desiring forgiveness. It is an act of brokenness. It is an attitude of worship. It is deciding who is going to be in charge of your life.

One afternoon a nine-year-old boy was visiting my office. His parents brought him so I could talk to him about becoming a Christian. During our time together I asked him if he knew the definition of "sin." He said he did, and he gave me his definition, which was very accurate. Then I asked him, "Do you sin?" He paused briefly to think about his answer and said, "I used to . . . but I gave it up." I wish I could do that. Just give it up. I am sure his mom, who was sitting out in my secretary's office, could think of some recent times that he had sinned, but for some reason, he could not. When children can't think of any sins that they have done, either they are caught off guard, they don't understand sin, or they have genuinely been obedient children for a few days (usually a child's strongest sense of sin is connected with breaking parental rules). However, the child who is serious about his relationship with God must face (confess) his sin and have a repentant heart.

After one Sunday morning worship service a mom told me that her son was ready to accept the Lord. I sat down next to him and began to talk. I could tell that he was sincere. As we continued to talk I asked him to talk to God about his decision. During his prayer he said to the Lord, "Dear Lord, forgive me for my sins," then paused and said, "and forgive my brother for his sins too. Lord, he does a lot of sins." Then he began to name some of these sins that his brother had recently done. I politely stopped him and asked him to focus on what he needed to tell God about himself instead of all the things his brother was doing wrong. Sometimes children can get a bit sidetracked, and you will need to help them stay focused.

Usually, when talking about sin, I ask children to tell me

about sins they have done or mention a couple that they struggle with the most. One afternoon a sweet young girl said to me, "I know I do, but right now I can't think of any." When a young child has a hard time identifying any sins he has committed, give him some examples (lying, unkind words, etc.) to help recall a recent sin in his life.

Two fourth-grade boys at church were having a serious discussion when I passed them in the hallway. One grabbed me by the arm and said, "Pastor Murphy, would you help us? We are having a disagreement."

"What about?" I asked.

"Did Jesus die for our money?" he replied.

"What do you mean?" I asked.

"Last week Pastor Henry said that 'Jesus died for our *cents.*'" He had no clue what the word *sins* meant and substituted what he thought it sounded like the pastor had said.

Is the Child Serious About This Commitment?

Sometimes children can be silly, flippant, uninterested, and anything but serious when you want them to be. But becoming a Christian is serious business. As a child is contemplating the decision to become a Christian, he will eventually come to a point when it is very important to him.

Listen to how he talks about becoming a Christian. Is there an urgency on his part? Does he have a personal desire to talk about salvation? Sometimes children who are familiar with the Christian language or have been raised in a Christian environment have an attitude of "Sure, why not," "I guess so," or "It sounds like a good idea to me." This may be a sign that the child has not reached a time of conviction. When a child is serious about his commitment to Christ, he should have an attitude of "I need to do this. I must ask Christ to come into my life." Do not confuse a child's impatience to be baptized with the seriousness of accepting Christ.

Is the Child's Decision Self-made?

It is not unusual for a child's salvation decision to be strongly connected to someone else, like a friend, relative, teacher, or pastor. Such a child may decide to become a Christian because he wants to please an important person in his life. Or the child wants to become a Christian because a friend, sibling, or cousin became a Christian.

Ask yourself the following questions:

- Does the child demonstrate a personal desire to make this commitment with his life, or is he just being agreeable with those around him who want him to become a Christian?
- Is he influenced to make this decision because his family or friends have already done this?
- Does he feel left out of the family or peer group?
- Is this a way of getting some undivided attention or public recognition?
- Is this decision a result of a need to feel loved or appreciated?
- Does he have a mature understanding of this decision?
- Are there signs that the child has personally struggled about this?
- Has the child expressed that he has reached this decision after a personal evaluation of his life?
- What influenced him the most to make this choice?
- Has his decision come after realizing how much he needs and wants Jesus in his life?

God will use the influence of others in our lives to bring us to Him. However, we don't want a child to make his choice to accept Christ for the sole purpose of pleasing those around him.

Has the Child's Decision Been Sealed?

When a child reaches the point of understanding, maturity, conviction, and desire to accept Christ, he needs to have a time and place to make this choice. You want him to remember the date and place of his spiritual birth if at all possible. If he had an earlier experience when he prayed to receive Christ, try to determine if it was a true conversion experience or just the beginning of his spiritual journey. Did his life begin to change then, or did his interest begin?

Many times I have met with children who have been talked to and prayed for by parents, teachers, friends, relatives, and pastors but have never been given the chance to make the choice for themselves. Adults have talked about becoming a Christian, but no one has explained how to do it. They may have repeated a prayer during one of those encounters, but they did not understand or remember what was prayed.

When a child is prepared to make a true decision for Christ, lead him to do so. Help the child put into his own words a prayer asking Christ into his life. Make sure he expresses conviction, repentance of sin, faith in Jesus, and a choice to receive Him. If he accidentally omits a significant part, gently coach him by reminding him to add that part and continue his prayer. When he has finished, you and others who are present should pray for him. Thank God for his decision and ask Him to bless him.

WHAT ARE SOME SIGNS THAT YOUR CHILD MAY NOT BE READY?

Is your child at the age where he believes in Santa Claus, the Easter Bunny, or the Tooth Fairy? Even if you don't acknowledge these pretend characters in your home, he may still find it difficult to separate "make-believe" from what is real. This may mean he is still in the "pretend" stage and not the "faith" stage. Does he seem to understand that make-believe is not real? Or does he talk about Peter Rabbit, Mother Goose, or Bambi as though they lived next door? If he can recognize that Peter Rabbit is fiction (though an enjoyable pretend friend) and Jesus is real, he's growing in readiness for mature faith.

If your child is at the pretend stage, don't discourage him from following Jesus; just keep teaching him until he can see the difference between the real and the pretend. Avoid going public with his decision until this is settled.

I asked a seven-year-old, "What is the difference between Jesus and Santa Claus?" He thoughtfully answered, "Jesus can walk through walls, but Santa has to use a chimney."

Remember, maturity and sincerity work together. One without the other weakens the decision.

Once a mom told me that her two-year-old "prayed the prayer." God is sovereign and can save anyone at any age He chooses, but from what we have observed about children, the probability of her child being "saved" was small. Instead of being saved the child was still "safe" and not even aware of being lost. Preschoolers and young children decide to become Christians much like they want to become doctors, policemen, or firemen. We don't discourage children at this age from their interest in becoming Christians. We realize that time will tell and continue pointing them in the right direction.

Young children usually demonstrate a love for God or interest in God as their first sign of spiritual interest. Conviction and repentance will usually follow later. A child's initial desire to become a Christian is usually the result of one of the following rationales:

- "I love God and want to obey Him. My parents (or pastor) say that asking Jesus into my heart is the way I show that I love Him."
- "I don't want to go to hell when I die. I want to go to heaven."
- "My friend (or sibling) got baptized. I love God too. I should get baptized."
- "I have been really sad since Grandmother died. I want to go to heaven so I can see her."
- "Nobody seems to really notice me until I mention things about God. My friend got lots and lots of attention when he got baptized. I want to get baptized too. Maybe that will make my parents and teachers be really proud of me."

- "I don't understand everything about becoming a Christian, but I think it sounds like a good thing."
- "I am the only one in my family (or class) who is not a Christian. This makes me feel weird and left out."

Though these are the initial reactions of children and do not mean a child is ready to become a Christian, *they are great starting points and should not be ignored.* Though children can sometimes ask hard questions, their questions mean that they have an interest in the things of God. Do not be afraid of their questions. Instead, be excited. When your child begins to show an interest in becoming a Christian, your encouragement is just like saying, "Come on, follow me; I will help you." Parents who do not respond to their child's questions are saying to their child, "You're on your own, kid; good luck."

HOW WILL I KNOW MY CHILD'S SPIRITUAL LEVEL?

By now you might have quite a few questions about how all this applies to your own child. So let me answer some of the questions that parents ask.

Q—If my child prayed the prayer to accept Christ, does that mean he is a Christian?

A—Not necessarily. It could, but it does not guarantee it. Some children pray this prayer fifty times before their spiritual lightbulb comes on. I have found that most children when praying their first prayer to accept Christ really are saying, "God, I am interested in becoming a Christian, but I don't understand it completely." If a young child wants to pray to accept Christ and you do not feel that he is completely ready, you might want to let him pray but make it clear that he should pray for Christ to *teach* him (not to *save* him). Young children are beginning to inquire. Parents who do not realize this will miss a great opportunity to help them grow to fully understand what being a Christian means.

Adults, too, often pray things that they don't mean or understand. We pray certain prayers out of habit, tradition, or because we have heard someone else pray that way. Sometimes we pray ignorantly without thinking about what we are saying.

Scripture never mentions a person "praying to receive Christ." But prayer is a very important part in most people's conversion experiences. It's the way we express our faith to God. Scripture does say, "Everyone who calls on the name of the Lord will be saved." *Praying the "right words" does not make him a Christian if he does not understand what he is saying.*

Asking someone from a different country to repeat the pledge to the American flag will not make him an American citizen. Some other events must take place as well.

Q—If my child is bright, will he accept Christ at an early age?

A—Maybe. But don't assume that he fully understands everything that he says. Children don't always mean what they say. Parents sometimes are fooled into thinking that since their child is advanced intellectually they do not need to teach him as much spiritually.

Even if a child prays at an early age to become a Christian, keep giving him lots of spiritual guidance. The mistake we make is when we stop helping the child grow after he has "prayed the prayer." As said earlier, that is the beginning of spiritual life, not the end goal.

Q—What does it mean if a child is asking lots of questions about becoming a Christian? Does that mean the child is ready?

A—I call this the spiritual kick in the womb. When a baby kicks his mother while he is still in the womb it is a sign that he is alive; though birth is near, it is not quite here. So it is when a child begins to ask questions or shows signs of desiring salvation. You know God is at work. Sometimes you or your child may wish that his spiritual birth would hurry up and come. But he may still be in the spiritual womb. Be sensitive and attentive. This spiritual kick in the womb means birth is around the corner. Be patient, and enjoy every moment. Remember, it is sometimes hard to tell the difference between false labor and real labor pains.

Parents will miss out on many of their child's better questions during this "kicking" stage if they don't know how to care for their child through this special time. Encouraging, listening, and discussing are so important.

I love it when children want to know about God. Their questions are so real, so honest. When your child starts asking questions about God, salvation, heaven, etc., don't be nervous. This is a wonderful time even if you don't know all the answers. Enjoy it. Use it to bring yourself and your child closer to God. Also, don't immediately assume that since your child is asking questions he is now ready to be saved or baptized. He may or may not be ready. As a matter of fact, children often stop asking those wonderful questions after they have been baptized because they think that it is the final part of becoming a Christian. So, do everything you can to field those questions and encourage more questions. Parents can help their child continue to grow after salvation and baptism by spending time each week discussing the Christian life and what the Bible says about it. Approach baptism as the birth announcement. Once your child has been baptized, continue to make time each week to disciple him. Parents who take time to walk through every stage will have children who make more mature, confident, long-lasting commitments.

Q—Am I going to harm my child's spiritual birth if I "hold him back"?

A—Yes and no.

Yes. If you hold him back from seeking to know and follow God, you will discourage him. If you treat him as if he is not good enough or smart enough, he will feel rejected. Salvation involves repentance and understanding. And none of us is "good enough" for salvation—that's the whole point! The Holy Spirit convicts us and helps us understand without rejecting us. We should be the same way when we are dealing with children.

Avoid blanket statements like "You are too young," "You don't know enough," "The church won't let you," or "You do too many bad things to be a Christian."

Instead, use encouraging words like "I am glad that you asked," or "God will teach you what that means, and I will help you too." If a young child says that he wants to pray to accept Christ, let him. Tell him that God will start showing him what it means to be a Christian. He may pray several times before he really understands what he is doing. But that is OK.

No. If you are positive with your child through each phase of his spiritual growth, you will only make his relationship with God stronger. Stretching out the time between his initial prayer of commitment and the time of baptism is wise. This can give a child time to see what God is doing in his life. Pausing gives you some time to look for changes in your child's life. It also helps him understand and enjoy baptism so much more. But make sure that you fill the time between a child's commitment to Christ and his baptism with activities that teach and encourage him.

Q—Our child grew up in church. How will that affect his readiness to accept Christ?

A—It depends. It depends on the church, your child's personality, and whether the Holy Spirit is actually drawing your child to repentance. Not all churches are child friendly. Dead churches can turn kids off to God. Your child may not see anything in the lives of those who attend church with him that would attract him to God.

But he will be exposed to more Christian terms and choices than other kids who do not attend church. He should have more questions about God earlier than kids who are unchurched.

Here is another result of his growing up in church. He may feel so comfortable in his Christian environment that he falsely thinks that he is already a Christian. Many times when I ask a child about his decision to become a Christian he says, "I have been a Christian all of my life." He will have to reach a point when he sees the difference between knowing about Christ and being a personal follower of Christ. While he is young he may not realize that he needs to make a personal commitment to Christ. However, he may want to do so because he hears the pastor mention it every week or because his family members are already Christians.

The key for every child is when someone personally connects with him to lead him to Christ. A personal counselor (parent, teacher, pastor, relative, friend, etc.) can determine if a child is just repeating concepts that are familiar to him or if he is going through a rebirth experience.

I realize that it is my responsibility as a father to lead my kids to Christ. However, I am thankful for the influence that pastors, teachers, and friends have made on my children.

Q—What if my child insists on joining the church, being baptized, or becoming a Christian?

A—Children are very impressionable. They are especially sensitive to the things their models tell them to do. If a child thinks his pastor or teacher expects him to be baptized, he will argue with his parents until they let him do it, even if the child does not have all of his facts straight. When a child insists on being baptized or joining the church, this may be because he hears the pastor each week invite people to do these things. He wants to obey his pastor. Sometimes it is hard to know if children are wanting to follow the Lord or just please us. So take time to evaluate. Children can be very persistent, and we do not want to hinder them from obeying the Lord. We just want to make sure they are doing it for the right reasons.

A child may be attracted to baptism or church membership because they are physical demonstrations of obeying God. His concrete-thinking mind has a difficult time comprehending abstract things like conviction, the Holy Spirit, or conversion.

When your child insists on responding in one of these ways, find out why. Let him know that you will be there to help him and guide him, just as you were there at his birth and when he learned to walk or ride a bike, and just as you will be when he begins to learn to drive a car, gets a job, or gets married. Remind him not to be impatient. We usually miss some great lessons when we are impatient. Look for some of the signs that your child is approaching a possible heart change, like conviction, humility, obedience, sensitivity, restlessness, or a battle between right and wrong. When children who have lived what we classify as "innocent lives" begin to see themselves as God does, they will begin to feel convicted.

When your child shows interest in such things, ask yourself if your child is going through a personal time of conviction or just being impatient. Remember to separate joining the church, or being baptized, from becoming a Christian. It is very normal for young children to want to follow their parents' or church leaders' example. They usually want to please us more than they want to please God. That is the way God designed it.

Q—What if a child cannot remember when, how, or where he became a Christian?

A—Becoming a Christian is a gradual process for many. However, once a person has repented from his old life and turned in the opposite direction, that person and others should notice a significant difference. The Bible calls this "conversion" (see Acts 15:3). Try to help pinpoint in your child's life when the change occurred. If there has not been any significant change or he cannot remember much about it, then the chances are he has not completed the spiritual birthing process. He may be close, and you may be able to induce him a little. He may not be ready at all, and you will have to encourage him to keep learning about Christ until he begins to understand. Do not go ahead and baptize a child when you are unsure.

When I counsel a child who is professing salvation, I usually ask him if he has changed any since becoming a Christian. Most will answer "yes" and give examples. It is helpful to recall the events leading up to his decision, how his decision occurred, and what has happened since.

Q—How much should I be involved in my child's decision to accept Christ? Should I leave it totally up to him, or do I let him know when I think he is ready?

A—Only your child can decide whether or not he will belong to Christ. You cannot make that decision for him. But do not abandon him while he is making this decision. No matter what he says or thinks, he needs your wisdom, and he needs your direction. Hold his hand throughout the whole process. Never say, "Whatever you want to do, Honey. It is up to you." Instead, say, "I am glad that you want to obey God. God will teach you what you need to understand about becoming a Christian. It will take a little time. Be patient. He has a plan for you. He will teach you one step at a time. We will know when He is ready for you to become a Christian. I will be here to help you each step of the way." Be involved in your child's decision to become a Christian. Lead him from the time he begins expressing an interest or has questions through his complete conversion experience.

Q—What if my child is shy or afraid? What if he is afraid to do anything publicly? How do I help him overcome his fear of going public or being baptized?

A—Tell him that you will be with him. Remind him that the public confession (baptism) is like a birth announcement. You might tell him, "This is one way we let others know that we really love Jesus. God does not want us to be secret Christians. It is our first act of bravery as a Christian. We all get nervous about being in front of others, and God knows that. God made us this way so it would remind us to trust Him. He will give you the courage if you ask Him and trust Him." Help the child feel more comfortable by arranging an appointment with the pastor prior to baptism. We will talk more about baptism in chapter 8.

Q—I understand how important it is to spend time nurturing and teaching our young children. But what should I do if my child is old enough to become a Christian and he has not done so?

A—Stay close to God and stay close to your child. If you believe he is old enough to understand, it is time to start teaching him the importance of making a personal decision to trust and follow Jesus. You still must leave this up to God, for many children are not ready until they are ten, eleven, or twelve years old. However, put together a team of teachers or friends who will also look for opportunities to talk about Christ with your child. Do not bombard or ambush him. Ask them if they see any signs that he is interested, convicted, or struggling with the issue of salvation. Occasionally discuss with him God's plan for our lives and explain the plan of salvation. See if he understands. Ask, "Have you been thinking about giving your life to Jesus?" "How does someone know if he is ready?" "Do you plan to give your life to Jesus?" "When do you think you will do that?" "What keeps you from doing it?" "What questions do you have about becoming a Christian?"

Pray for him daily. Trust the Lord. Pray for wisdom for yourself. Make sure that your life is not a stumbling block for him in any way. God will honor your dependence on Him.

Do you know your child well enough to know what he is thinking about God? You are a wise parent, teacher, or counselor if you help the children in your life grow from their initial interest in God to a mature commitment of their lives to Him. The confusing or difficult part of this period for most parents is *knowing what to do from the time a child begins asking questions until he is ready to become a Christian.* Try to put the importance of your child's decision ahead of your frustration of not knowing exactly what to do. Spending time with your child is valuable to you and your child's spiritual maturity. Put at least as much emphasis on helping your child grow in Christ as on helping him make a decision about Christ.

Chapter Six
Leading Children to Christ

One of the greatest challenges in talking to children about salvation is the *language barrier*. When it comes to spiritual things we speak a completely different language than what we use for everyday life. Christians have a special language with terms that come from God's Word or from our own Christian traditions and music. Much of what we say makes no sense to those who do not know Christ. It can be very unclear to those outside of the Christian family, and it is especially confusing to children.

Teaching children the Christian language is not our goal. Teaching them to choose the Christian life is. Think before you speak. Be careful what you say to children. They take everything so literally and are easily confused with our symbolic, religious terminology. And when they do not understand the words, they often substitute more familiar words that sound like the ones they heard.

THE CHURCH ENGLISH

An Asian mother who had recently moved to America with three boys had been attending our church. Each time I spoke to her she covered her mouth as she spoke. She was struggling with English and felt embarrassed. One morning when I greeted her I bragged on her English and asked, "How are your boys doing with their English?"

She told me, "They do very good, but do not understand church English." There is a lesson here for us.

Each of the churches where I have served offers a time of commitment at the close of the worship services. At this time those who have questions, need counseling, want prayer, or wish to make some type of commitment to Christ are invited to walk toward the pulpit area where they are greeted by a pastor or counselor. During this time I look for any children who might want to talk to someone. When I greet a child during this special time I usually introduce myself, ask the child's name, and say something like, "How can I help you?" or "Do you have a question or something you want to tell me?" Their responses are always precious, but many times they can be quite humorous. Here are some examples of how children sometimes get confused or have difficulty expressing themselves regarding spiritual things.

Which Organ Is It?

At the end of one of our morning worship services during the public invitation to accept Christ, a young girl came to me for some spiritual help. In a nervous voice she blurted out, "I want to ask Jesus into my stomach." Though she had not used the more familiar term "heart," I knew she was broken over her sinful condition and desired to follow Christ with her life.

What About Moses?

Another little girl (first or second grade) came forward at the close of the service. I soon discovered that she had not attended our church very long. When I greeted her she said something like this: "I want to ask Jesus into my heart, but can I ask Moses too? I know him a lot better." She had attended Sunday school the past two or three weeks and, you guessed it, the lessons had been about Moses.

Chairman of the Demons

Randle was often hilarious without meaning to be. Almost everything he said was quotable. One Sunday afternoon as I was sitting down to eat lunch, his mom called. She had a concern about something Randle had been taught in Sunday school that day. "Today, when Randle came home from church he said to me, 'Mom, when I grow up I want to be a demon.'"

Without informing her that he was already off to a good start, I asked, "Where did he get that idea?"

"I think he got it in Sunday school. When I asked, 'Randle, what do you mean you want to be a demon when you grow up?' he said, 'You know, Mom, one of those men who sit down front and take up the offering.'" Of course, he meant to say "deacon."

Bride of Christ

I had the blessing of growing up in a home where I was taken to church from the time I was a baby. But I don't remember hearing of "the bride of Christ" until I was in junior high school. When my pastor mentioned that Jesus will be coming for His bride, my first thought was that since God had picked a mother for Jesus He was going to pick a wife for Him too. I didn't know that His "bride" was the church.

Open Up Your Heart

A story that has been passed around for years through children's ministry circles is about a mom and her young son on their way home from church. The boy asked the question, "Mom, how does someone become a Christian?"

"They invite Jesus to come into their heart," she said.

"Does it hurt?" he responded.

"Not at all. I've done it. All you do is open up your heart and He comes in," she told him.

When they arrived home the mom went to her room to change clothes. When she went into the kitchen to prepare their lunch she was horrified. There was her son with a large knife preparing to "open up his heart" to Jesus.

LEARNING TO COMMUNICATE

Sometimes we have the best intentions but don't stop to listen to the answers or explanations we give our children. It should be our goal to help a child understand by using terms that he can comprehend. *Avoid using symbolic terms* or phrases that can confuse a child. Churchy language does not just confuse children; it can also confuse adults who are not part of the Christian faith. Here are some examples of religious terms that either confuse, mislead, or have no meaning at all to children.

- *"Profession of faith"*
- *"Washed in the blood"*
- *"Take the pastor's hand"*
- *"Crucified with Christ"*
- *"Die to self"*
- *"Justified by faith"*
- *"Buried with him in baptism"*
- *"Open up your heart"*
- *"Being born again"*

Children do need to learn some of "the language of the church." However, not all phrases are equally important. Church phraseology fall into several categories: (a) "churchy" language that is grounded in tradition rather than Scripture, (b) biblical terms that a person should understand at some point but that are certainly not basic for salvation, (c) language that is important, but theologically dense and probably more appropriate for adults, and (d) language that is essential and needs to be explained to children: *sin, faith, repentance, baptism, salvation,* etc. (and any other unfamiliar terms that come up in songs or Scripture verses you are teaching children).

TALKING TO CHILDREN ABOUT GOD

Even those who are experienced in discussing their faith need to stop and think before talking with children. A friend of mine who has led many people to know the Lord told me that one day she was talking to a child about trusting Jesus and she asked the question, "What are the requirements to become a Christian?"

To her surprise the child answered, "What are 'requirements'?" Words that are familiar to us can be puzzling to children. The language we use with our children should be simple, elementary English. Use one- and two-syllable words if possible.

When children begin to pick up Christian terms they hear us use, we sometimes assume that they understand them. Even adults use Christian terms that they do not fully understand. I gave some questions on p. 78 to help you determine whether or not your child is ready to become a Christian.

When talking to a child about God, make sure you get feedback so you can tell if he hears what you are trying to say. Don't assume that because a child can state the facts of becoming a Christian or uses Christian vocabulary that he truly understands what he needs to know. Salvation is more than a good vocabulary. Children as young as two years old can begin to use Christian terms or memorize prayers.

The vocabulary and knowledge of today's child is rather amazing. Children today are exposed to large amounts of information. They may seem to be smarter than we were at their age. Don't be fooled if a child talks as though he is an adult; he is still a child. A child who seems comfortable using religious phrases can appear to be more spiritually mature than he actually is. Look past the vocabulary and find out what the child thinks and feels. When a child gives the impression that he is ready to receive Christ, we are tempted to lead him in prayer and send him on his way without really determining his level of understanding. When we release him from our care too quickly, we rob him of spiritual growth.

Do children get saved earlier if they are smarter? Salvation is not based on intelligence alone, is it? Should today's young people get married earlier because they know more? No. Should we allow teens to get their driver's licenses earlier because they have more information? Of course not. Don't overreact to how a child does or does not respond verbally. Look inside the child as well as outside. There is much joy in discovering what is inside a child, but that takes time. And it should.

Increasing Your Confidence

Three things will help us become more confident when talking to children about salvation. First, good communication takes *training.* Just because you are able to have children does not automatically qualify you to be a good parent. You must learn to be a good parent. Read good books about Christian parenting. Seek advice from other godly parents you know. Talk with pastors and children's leaders about your child. Attend Christian parenting conferences.

The Bible does not talk much about children becoming Christians. That's because there is only one way to become a Christian; there is not one way for adults and another way for children. A child must do what anyone else does when accepting Christ as Savior and the Lord of his life. If a child loves Jesus and says that he believes in Him, but has not been broken or repentant of sin, then he is about halfway through the spiritual birth process. Being trained to look for these signs of readiness greatly increases a parent's confidence.

Parents and churches make the mistake of letting children believe they are Christians when they have not experienced the whole birthing process. Do not deceive your children in this way. Encourage them in their first steps and tell them (in a positive way) that there is even more to come. Be with them during the process. Do not leave them all alone to guess their way through.

Walk along the journey with them.

The Bible commands parents to teach their children the principles from God's Word. No good parents would want to leave their children's salvation to chance. Study what the Bible says about children, fathers, mothers, marriage, and so forth. Then you will have a strong foundation for the other things God will teach you later. That you are reading this book shows that you want to be the best equipped parent, pastor, or children's leader that you can be.

Second, building your confidence takes *time*. The more you involve yourself with children, the better understanding you will have of children. The more you talk to kids in general, the more comfortable you will become. Teaching or helping in a children's Sunday school class provides valuable experience. Lois Ann and I both have degrees in childhood education, but the experience we have had teaching and working with children has been one of the most valuable helps for us as parents. I have known several parents to teach Sunday school partly in order to become better parents.

I encourage you to get involved in the lives of children. They need you, and you need them. Become active in the children's ministry programs where you and your children attend church. It saddens me when I see parents who have made time to volunteer for Little League, scouting, school activities, and everything else, but have not made time for their child's spiritual or church life. This speaks volumes to children about what their parents value the most. Make time for children, and God will help you gain confidence in relating to them.

Explaining the gospel to children also takes *trust*. You must trust God's Holy Spirit to do His part and help you do yours. Trusting does not mean that you are leaving everything up to God. God has commanded us to be a big part of the shaping of our children's spiritual lives. I really am glad that He included us. His Spirit is all powerful and all knowing. He does not need us but wants to use us. What a joy that is.

The closer you get to your children, the more sensitive you will be to their needs. The closer you get to God, the more sensitive you will be to His Spirit's leading. Pray. Pray for your child that he or she will make a strong commitment to Christ. Pray for yourself that you will be sensitive to what your child needs from you. Pray that God will use you in leading your child to Him. Ask God to help you live a life that is pleasing to Him and a model to your child.

Increasing Your Knowledge

No one who loves children wants to mishandle how he leads them to Christ. We do not want to push children when they are not ready. Neither do we want to hold them back from seeking God though they are young. Either one of these reactions would be wrong. But we must purpose in our hearts that we are going to do everything within our influence to lead our children to a strong relationship with Jesus. This is our highest calling and greatest reward as parents and children's leaders.

Leading children to Christ is not something we have to be nervous about. Neither is it something we should enter into ignorantly. Most of us talk to children about the Lord the same way our parents or Sunday school teachers talked to us when we were children. But much has been learned the past twenty years about children and leading them to Christ.

Many of us received Christ and have a strong relationship with Him in spite of our parents' mistakes or lack of knowledge about children. Our parents did the best they could with what they knew. Today we are blessed to know so much more about children than our parents' generation did. Therefore, we should take advantage of this information.

You are not alone when you get an uncomfortable feeling while trying to talk to your child about the Lord. You may see your pastor as better qualified, as the "expert," but most pastors get that same nervous feeling when they talk to a child. Most pastors spend the majority of their time with adults, and their training is on the adult level. Therefore, when the occasion arises for them to talk to a child, they have a feeling of inadequacy. Usually, there are two issues on the pastor's mind: How do I determine and deal with the spiritual needs of this child, and how do I handle the expectations of the parent(s) involved?

If you are like most parents, you probably have not had many opportunities to lead children to Christ. In addition to the lack of experience on parents' part, children often catch parents off guard with their questions. These factors alone cause parents to feel a bit helpless or uneasy in their efforts.

That you have children, work with children, and/or love children does not automatically equip you to lead children to Christ. But it should give you a desire to do so.

Years ago I asked the Lord to help me understand how to lead children to Him. I am passing on to you what I have learned. At this writing I have baptized more than twelve hundred children. What a tremendous education this has been for me. God has been so good to me. I don't know everything about children and salvation. But I want to know as much as I can. I want to have the greatest influence on children's lives that I possibly can. I want to rescue as many as possible from hell and the grip of Satan.

I come from a medical family and was a pre-med student for a brief time in college. I have come to realize that there are two very important components in medicine. It is important that physicians have the best training. This will determine their level of excellence. Their ability to diagnose an illness and their surgical technique are both the outcome of proper training. However, another factor is important to the medical condition of the patient: the patient's general health. Patients who practice a life of good health do not have to rely solely on the doctor's expertise. Their bodies provide them with a head start.

Do you see the implication here? We focus so much on the technique of leading children to Christ that we overlook the child's spiritual health. Although technique is very important, children raised in a healthy spiritual environment are more likely to trust the Lord than those who are not raised that way.

Remember this: God is the *obstetrician,* and we are the *pediatricians.* He takes care of the birth. We help with the baby's growth. He alone gives spiritual birth. He expects us to provide spiritual health. We are to lead, guide, feed, and help this baby Christian grow, but only He can save a child. What a privilege it has been to be involved in the salvation of my two sons. What a blessing it is to lead boys and girls to faith in Christ.

What if you have done everything that you know to do but you are still not sure if your child is ready to accept Christ? Turn it over to God. Ask the Holy Spirit to help you. Also ask others who know your child for advice. Form a team of spiritual advisers. Don't pressure your child out of your own frustration or impatience. Be faithful and patient; God's timing is perfect. And don't stop discussing, communicating, teaching, and encouraging.

Witnessing to Children

I am often asked, "What pamphlet, tract, or witnessing tool do you recommend to use when explaining the gospel to children?"

One problem in selecting a witnessing tool for children is that it is difficult to find a single gospel tract that could be appropriate for children of all ages. Most tracts explain the steps to becoming a Christian and ask the reader to pray a prayer of commitment. But most tracts do not help the one who is witnessing to the child know what that child needs or what he does not quite understand. Preschoolers and preteens are miles apart spiritually, emotionally, and intellectually. We should approach each child in an age-appropriate way and in a way that fits that individual child. Tracts can provide a starting point, but they usually do not involve enough discussion.

The steps to salvation are the same for all ages. The gospel message is the same. But children's understanding varies. *The purpose of this book is to prepare you to present the gospel to children of all ages.*

Testing the Child's Readiness

Matthew 13 tells us that the Word of God falls on different types

98

of soil. Some soil is ready for the seed to take root and grow, whereas other types of soil are not. The passage describes five soil types.

Beaten path—This soil is hard from being trampled on. It is also dry. Seeds cannot grow in this type of soil. Some children are emotionally beaten down and dry from the discouraging or abusive atmosphere in which they live. The stress in life has hardened them.

Rocky soil—This soil has foreign objects in it that must be removed. Children may have issues in their lives (e.g., personal sins, divorce, death, illness, abuse) that must first be dealt with before we can witness effectively.

Shallow soil—In this soil seeds spring up quickly but do not take root. A child can be enthusiastic about following Christ but can quickly become discouraged by the challenges that will come his way. Every child needs personal follow-up once he has shown an interest in becoming a Christian.

Thorny soil—Weeds will choke other plants that try to grow. Children who are "choked" by their surroundings need a place to go where they can hear about Christ and learn from God's Word without fear of ridicule. They also need someone who will cultivate them, someone who will pull out the weeds that spring up to choke them. Today's weeds may include negative peer pressure, television, family issues, and other cultural snares.

Good soil—This soil is fertile and ready for planting. Most soil can eventually become fertile if we do what it takes to prepare it. It is the same way with the faith of a child. If we will prepare a child's heart to believe and receive the good news of Christ, God will do the rest.

This parable of the sower does not tell us much about the sower. It tells about the types of soil. The sower might feel like sowing, but unless the soil is prepared, he is wasting his time. Every farmer who knows anything about farming knows that it takes more time to prepare the soil than it does to plant. Once the seed is planted you do not leave it, but you go back and cultivate, kill weeds, water it, fertilize it, and otherwise nurture the young plants. We do not always know what type of soil we are going up against. Therefore, we must do more than just scatter seed. We must spend time in the dirt.

Understanding the Process

The process of planting and harvesting goes something like this:

1. till
2. plant
3. fertilize
4. water
5. cultivate
6. harvest

It is largely a parent's job to build a strong little Christian who grows up into a strong big Christian. The principle of the soil is so important. The way we communicate to a child depends on his type of soil and the amount of preparation of that soil. Sometimes it is very difficult or even impossible to know the condition of the soil (soul) in the life of every child with whom we come in contact. We want to sow every time we get a chance, but if we just sow and never till, water, fertilize, or cultivate, we may just choke or drown the soil and get nothing in return. If you want to see a child accept Christ, then you must first discover what condition his soil is in. If you prepare and cultivate his heart, then the seeds you plant for Christ are more likely to grow.

How do children become Christians? They accept Christ the same way that anyone does. As mentioned before, there is no set of "junior rules" just for children. Children do not become Christians by partially accepting Jesus Christ as their Savior.

What are the different components of salvation?

1. conviction
2. repentance
3. faith
4. commitment

Have you ever talked to a child who believed everything about Jesus but just did not seem to be convicted? His approach seemed to be "Why not believe in Jesus? It sounds like the right thing to do." Have you ever observed a child who was deeply convicted about his sin and wanted God in his life? If you have had the benefit of talking with both types of children you have noticed how different they are. This is why it is important to know the different spiritual needs that children have.

Using Scriptures That Explain Salvation

What Scriptures are good to use when talking to children?

John 3:16—"For God so loved the world that he gave his one and only Son, that whoever believes in him shall not perish but have eternal life."

Romans 3:23—"For all have sinned and fall short of the glory of God."

Romans 6:23—"For the wages of sin is death, but the gift of God is eternal life in Christ Jesus our Lord."

Romans 5:8—"But God demonstrates his own love for us in this: While we were still sinners, Christ died for us."

Romans 10:9–10, 13—"That if you confess with your mouth, 'Jesus is Lord,' and believe in your heart that God raised him from the dead, you will be saved. For it is with your heart that you believe and are justified, and it is with your mouth that you confess and are saved . . . for, 'Everyone who calls on the name of the Lord will be saved.'"

Note: John 3:16 may be all you need. If you use more than two or three Scriptures, you will need to review or summarize what you have read when you finish. It is too much for a young mind to remember. Take time to explain the unfamiliar words (e.g., perish, wages, demonstrates, confess, justified).

COUNSELING YOUR CHILDREN ABOUT SALVATION

What is the role of a counselor? A counselor plays the part of adviser, guide, coach, mentor, teacher, and helper. A counselor may be a parent, relative, teacher, pastor, or anyone who has an opportunity to talk to a child about becoming a Christian. The counselor is an encourager, explainer, explorer, listener, and nurturer. Here are some helps that will assist you as you counsel your child about becoming a Christian.

Be Natural and at Ease

Relax. Don't worry about saying everything just right. Find a private place to talk where there are no distractions. This will help everyone focus and relax.

Find out what questions or intentions the child may have. The child may not know what he needs or wants. He may have a slight interest in becoming a Christian or a deep conviction about it. Watch his body language. Is he nervous, tired, shy, bored?

Don't forget to pray before and during your meeting with the child. Pray and ask the Holy Spirit to give you the right words to say.

Don't Be Rushed

It can take less than ten minutes to get a child to make the "decision" to become a Christian. But helping him to fully understand may take longer. Take time to get to know the child's needs and his level of understanding. Do not be in a hurry. Spend time listening and praying for God's leadership. Give the child time to think, absorb, and react.

Find Out What the Child Is Thinking

Here is a sampling of introductory questions to help you discover what a child might be thinking. They will vary depending on the age of the child, the location of the conversation, and your church affiliation.

- "Are you thinking about becoming a Christian (or giving your life to Jesus, following Jesus with your life)? Why? What made you start thinking about doing that?"
- "How old were you when you began to start thinking about becoming a Christian? Where and when did this take place?"
- "Has anyone ever explained to you how to become a Christian?"
- "What is a Christian?" "Why do want to become a Christian?" "How does someone become a Christian?" "How can you tell if someone is a Christian?"
- "Why do you want to get baptized?" "Why do people get baptized?"
- "Are you already a Christian, still thinking about it, or not really sure?"
- "What does that mean to you?" (used repeatedly throughout conversation)
- "Does what I just said make sense to you?" (used repeatedly throughout conversation)
- "What is it that you do not understand about becoming a Christian or giving your life to Jesus?"
- "What questions do you want to ask me?"

Encourage the Child to Express Himself in His Own Words

If he uses "churchy" or religious terms, ask him to explain what those terms mean in words that are easier to understand.

Many times children will express a desire to "ask Jesus into their hearts," but when asked to explain what that means they have a very difficult time. Ask the child to explain it as if he were talking to a friend his age who did not go to church. If or when he struggles, stop and help. You may need to explain it for him or give some hints throughout the conversation. When you have finished, ask him to repeat to you what you have just discussed. Let him know that you do not expect perfect answers.

Be Quiet and Listen

When adults get nervous they talk too much. It is normal for an adult to spend 90 percent of a conversation talking and only 10 percent listening. Don't ask a child questions that only ask for "yes" or "no" answers. Ask questions that ask for explanation. Let children talk. Hear what they are thinking instead of trying to get them to agree with everything you are saying.

Explore Until You Find the Child's Spiritual Maturity Level

Refer back to the four stages of spiritual development that were discussed earlier (pages 59–66). It will help tremendously if you memorize these four categories.

At this point in the conversation I usually review with every child three things that a person must do if he wants to become a Christian. These will be presented in the next section.

Simply Explain God's Plan

Read John 3:16 together with the child. Summarize it in this way: "God loves you. But your sin keeps you from God and deserves punishment. Your punishment is to be separated from God in hell forever. God sent Jesus to forgive you, to take your punishment, and to give you the gift of eternal life. To receive forgiveness and eternal life you must admit that you are a sinner and need God's forgiveness. You must believe that Jesus is the Son of God and must choose Him as your Lord and Savior.

"There are three things you must do to become a Christian."

Admit (Repentance). "First, you must realize that you have a problem. Each of us has a problem. What is it? It is sin. Sin keeps us from being close to God. It separates us from God."

A child must take a step further than just knowing what sin is. He must realize that he has sinned and be ashamed of his sin. He must desire and seek God's forgiveness. He must humbly and sincerely confess that he is a sinner. He must be grateful that Jesus took the punishment for his sins. That is why Jesus died on the cross. Each of us must repent of sin (turn away from it) to become a Christian.

"Admit that you have a problem. What are you going to do about your sin?"

Believe (Faith). "Second, believe in Jesus. Jesus is more than just some special person in history that we mention from time to time. Faith is not just believing that Jesus once lived on the earth. Faith is believing that Jesus is the Son of God. Faith is believing that Jesus was God in a human body. Faith is believing that Jesus is alive and real today."

Jesus was killed because He told people about God and because He said He was God. But on the third day after He died, He came back to life. Jesus rose from the dead. Now He lives in heaven with God and lives in our lives if we invite Him to do so. Believe that Jesus loves you and came to earth to tell us about God. Believe that you can trust Him. Love and trust Jesus.

"What do you believe about Jesus?"

Choose (Promise). "Third, we must tell God what we understand about the first two things and ask Him to come into our lives to be the ruler, master, and teacher of our lives. In other words, we accept His gift of salvation and give our lives to Him."

"Are you ready to receive God's gift of eternal life and give your life to God?"

Leave the Decision Up to the Child

He may already feel that if he doesn't go through with it that you will be hurt or mad or that you will be greatly disappointed. You do not want a child to be confused between following Christ and pleasing you. Take the pressure off of him by letting him know that you will love him no matter what he does and that you just want to help him understand. Remind him that he should not make this decision just because you are a Christian.

Encourage the Child

If the child is not ready to accept Christ (he's immature, does not understand, or is not under conviction), convey to him that you are glad that he is learning what it means to become a Christian. Remind him that God will show him all that he needs to know when God knows he is ready. Encourage the child to wait on the Lord and to learn from you (his parents) and teachers. Tell him that any time he wants, he can talk with you or make an appointment to talk with the pastor or church staff to ask questions.

If the child is ready, ask him to pray and make his decision right now. Ask him to put the prayer in his own words.

When in doubt about a child's readiness, don't run ahead; take a step back. Take time to feed, grow, nurture, encourage, examine, and teach that child. Ask those who know your child for their opinions.

Pray with the Child

In most cases I do not ask a child to repeat after me during his prayer for salvation. I ask him to say it in his own words. If he needs help or forgets something that should be included, then I pick it up at that point. If a child is very shy I may ask him to repeat after me.

COUNSELING OTHER PEOPLE'S CHILDREN ABOUT SALVATION

What if the child you are talking with is not your child? It may take longer to find out what his spiritual level is, and what questions he has. In addition to the previous suggestions, I have found several guidelines to be helpful when I deal with other people's children.

Talk with the Child's Parents

Talk privately with the child's parents if possible before you begin visiting with the child. They can help you by telling what experiences or questions the child has had prior to this time. This may be a fresh experience for their child or something they have discussed with the child for several months. After a few minutes of discussion, ask the parents to give you a few minutes alone with the child so you can spend time getting to know him. Ask the parents to spend this time in prayer for you and their child. Encourage them to list any questions that they might have as well. Having this private time with the child helps take the pressure off the child, the parents, and you.

Get to Know the Child

Next, begin finding out some basic information about the child. What is the child's age? What is his church or religious background? Was he raised in a Christian home? Has he been thinking about this decision to follow Christ for a long time or a short period of time? Has he ever discussed becoming a Christian with his parents, teachers, relatives, or friends?

One of my favorite ways to discover a child's spiritual maturity level is through role-playing. This is not a new counseling method. It has been tested and tried for a long time. Most of the time role-playing helps a child relax. It takes the focus off of him and puts it somewhere else. Here is an example of how to use role-playing to find a child's spiritual awareness.

Me—"Johnny, who is one of your best friends?"

Johnny—"Michael."

Me—"Pretend I am Michael, OK? And one day I came to you and said, 'I have a problem and I don't know what to do. Would you help me?'"

Johnny—"OK."

Me—"I have been thinking about becoming a Christian, but

I am not sure what a Christian is. What is a Christian?"

Johnny's answer will usually fall into one of the following categories:

a. Believes in Jesus, repents of his sin, commits his life to Christ

b. Does good works, attends church, has good behavior, reads Bible, prays

Me—"Thanks. Now, let me ask you another question. It might help me if you can tell me if anything like this has happened to you. Have you already become a Christian, are you still thinking about it, or are you just not quite sure?"

Johnny—

a. If he is unsure or still thinking about it, find out why. Ask him what questions he has.

b. If he says he is already a Christian, ask him to tell you how it happened. "Where were you when you became a Christian? What happened?"

Me—

a. If he is unsure, I will help him retrace his steps, review what the Bible says someone must do to become a Christian, remind him that he does not have to ask Christ for salvation over and over if he really understands what it means. My goal is to either help him realize that he has already made a commitment to Christ, or lead him to do so, if I feel that he is ready.

b. If he has already become a Christian, then I will talk to him about obedience, growth, faithfulness, and baptism.

Follow Through with the Family

When the child is ready to accept Christ, invite the parents to join you. Review with them what you and the child have discussed and discovered. You may need to do this privately with the parents. They may have questions, or they may need the Lord too. Give the child the choice of going home and praying with his parents and family or praying right now with you.

Follow up with the family in a few days. Check back with the child in a few days to see if he is growing, if he has questions, and if he has talked with his parents. Talk with his parents and see if they are supporting his decision. Be sure to verify whether they faithfully attend church or need an invitation to do so.

How should we witness to children? With genuine love. With nonthreatening questions. With English, not religious/symbolic language. And with patience and sensitivity.

Chapter Seven
The Roles of Parents and Teachers

$\mathcal{W}$e have looked at what it takes to lead a child to Christ, but how do you prepare for that time? How do you instill a Christian worldview in your children and conduct your family life in a way that pleases Christ? Or, if you are a teacher, what can you do to be better prepared to lead children to the Savior? In this chapter, we'll look at those questions.

THE ROLE PARENTS HAVE IN LEADING THEIR CHILDREN TO CHRIST

Parents' Primary Obligations

The good news is that Scripture says a lot about a parent's responsibility toward his or her children. The bad news is that nowhere does it indicate this is a quick or easy job. What are some duties given to parents?

Train them. Proverbs 22:6 says, "Train a child in the way he should go, and when he is old he will not turn from it."

Instruct them. Ephesians 6:4 says, "Fathers, do not exasperate your children; instead, bring them up in the training and instruction of the Lord."

Manage your household. First Timothy 3:4 gives the obligations of an overseer or elder, which sets a good standard for any father. "He must manage his own family well and see that his children obey him with proper respect."

Encourage your children. Colossians 3:21 says, "Fathers, do not embitter your children, or they will become discouraged."

Impress God's truths on your family. Deuteronomy 6:4–7 says,

> Hear, O Israel: The Lord our God, the Lord is one. Love the Lord your God with all your heart and with all your soul and with all your strength. These commandments that I give you today are to be upon your hearts. Impress them on your children. Talk about them when you sit at home and when you walk along the road, when you lie down and when you get up.

I love this passage. It says that *parents* are the ones who have the responsibility of teaching their children about God. The impression parents make stays with children for their entire lifetime. God's Word gives us *four natural times each day* when parents have the opportunity to teach their children about God. We will take a closer look at these later.

Christian parenting is a full-time job. It starts from the time a child rises in the morning until he lies down at night. If you are a parent, you are the greatest influence in your child's life. You may not think so because of all the other things that grab at your child, but you are the most important.

Your concern should not only be "When will my child be ready to accept Christ?" but also, "What will I do before, during, and after the process to securely lead my child to a real relationship with Christ?" We must decide that, in spite of the rush brought on by life's demands, we will take the time to build the lives around us, especially our children. This takes commitment and dependence on God.

Young Timothy was taught from the time he was an infant, and he grew to be a wise young man who was strong in the Lord. Don't wait until your child begins to ask questions or show an interest in the things of God. Take the lead in your child's spiritual training. Think ahead how you will lead your child to Christ.

Excellent Teaching Times

Take time to teach your children about God. Deuteronomy 6:7 says that there are four basic teaching times in each day.

Rising up. This is the way you start your child's day. What is the first thing your child hears you say each morning? What is his first impression of the day? Praise music, happy greetings, and family time at breakfast are ways to start your child with a joyful morning. How your child starts the day is so important. Start each day with praise, Scripture, singing, prayer, encouragement, and togetherness. Focus on God the first thing each day.

Most families do not eat a sit-down breakfast each morning. They grab a bowl of cereal and pass each other as they rush to get ready. Make it a goal to spend a few minutes together as a family with the Lord each morning.

Lying down. This is how you end your child's day. What is the last thing he hears you say at night? Do you have a nightly routine with God? Reading good books, reading or telling Bible stories, prayer time, and quiet music are good tools for closing out the day.

End each day with bedtime prayers and a devotion time. This is a time of thanksgiving to God and a time to evaluate the day. What were the good things for which you can praise God? What were the failures, challenges, and prayer concerns? Leave a little time for discussion. End the day on a positive note if at all possible. Remove any malice that may exist. Teach your child to end his day with thanksgiving.

Sitting at home. Most families don't come home and sit together. They come home and plop themselves down somewhere and crash. Setting aside a weekly family night is one way of keeping the family close. Talk, eat, play a game, spend time together.

Before the night is over, take the opportunity to teach a Bible story or biblical principle. Set aside time every week that says, "Our family is important." It is also a great time to focus on the Lord. The family night is a wonderful time for teaching, discussion, games, prayer, or making adjustments in schedules or rules.

Walking along the road. Each day we have opportunities to teach our children about God. These include daily and spontaneous circumstances. How we react to the events and challenges of our daily lives is a powerful teaching tool for our children.

Look for other times to teach your children about the Lord. As we "walk along the road" we have many opportunities to see God at work and to make choices to please Him.

Parents' Opportunities to Influence Their Children

Be a committed Christian. It is really important that parents understand how to talk to their children about becoming Christians, but it is more important that parents live godly lives. More is caught than taught. Exemplifying the fruits of the Spirit (Galatians 5—love, joy, peace, patience, kindness, goodness, faithfulness, gentleness, and self-control) is such a powerful testimony to your child (and anyone else, for that matter). God tells us to live that way whether or not we have children. We all know that actions speak a lot louder than words and that faith without works is dead. Make daily choices based on biblical truths. Ask yourself "What would Jesus do in this situation?" Spend personal time in prayer, Bible study, and spiritual growth. Have a prayer/accountability partner.

Have a good relationship with your children. Spend time together. Talk to each other. Have daily conversations about various topics. Many parents and children have trouble communicating and tend to misunderstand each other because they haven't built a strong communication system. They have not taken the time to know each other very well.

If you and your child don't spend enough time talking together about other things, it will weaken your discussions when it is time to talk to your child about becoming a Christian. Talking with your child gives you time to analyze many facets of his or her life (belief system, questions about God, fears, peer influence, etc.).

Parents who have developed a good talking relationship are better equipped to break the code barrier. Sometimes children say things in agreement with us out of fear that we will be disappointed or upset if they have a differing view. Other times they may say things in a negative fashion just to get our response, because they need our reassurance, or to let off steam.

Sometimes either the child or a parent tends to dominate conversations. Some children will talk our ears off about trivial topics. Some parents only talk when there is some serious topic or a lesson to be learned. Each of these is an example of one-way communication. Make sure that both parties are involved.

I have observed thousands of teachers through the years. One type I've noticed likes to lecture, never involving the students. This can be the result of a time limit allowed for the topic being taught or a teacher who has not discovered how to use better teaching styles. Educators learned long ago that lecture alone does not equal good teaching. Good teaching involves being connected with the student, not just giving facts to be memorized. Sometimes we sound like we are lecturing when we don't intend to do so. We do not want to lecture our children into becoming Christians; we want to lead them to do so.

Understanding your children helps you polish their strengths and also gives you goals for improving their weak areas. People with healthy relationships have discovered how to better handle conflict and hear what the other person is really saying or feeling. Remember, the goal in understanding your children is not to label them, but to understand them so you can improve your relationships.

Create a healthy, positive, Christian atmosphere in the home. One way to do this is by putting positive reminders or reinforcements in your home (Deuteronomy 6). Start your day with praise. End your day by praying together. Laugh together (which is not the same thing as teasing each other). Establish family nights and devotions.

Be prepared and alert. Look for opportunities to talk about Christ with your children. Prepare yourself

- spiritually—Repent of anything that would keep you from being a usable instrument or that would cause you to be a stumbling block. Be an example.
- physically—Keep yourself healthy. Exercise, rest, and eat right.
- mentally—Rehearse what you will say. Relax and trust God to guide you.

Attend a good church and Sunday school. If at all possible find a church that has a good children's ministry with age-graded activities and trained, godly leaders. That means it is a Bible-centered, loving, fun place that involves the children in learning activities. Don't just send your kids to Sunday school; attend an adult Bible study class yourself. Attend worship together as a family. Your church may provide child care for preschoolers during the worship time, but by the middle elementary years you should participate in worship as a family. These few years during your child's elementary years may be the only time you get to worship together. When your child becomes a teenager he may want to sit with his friends or youth leaders. Children grow up fast, so enjoy your worship time as a family while you can.

Choose Christian role models and heroes. All through history God has used special men and women as heroes of the faith to lead us and point us to Him. It is human nature to look for heroes. Your child will naturally seek heroes, but without your help he or she may have a hard time selecting people with godly character.

With all the media influences in our lives today we are bombarded with celebrity types. Many of these rich and famous people could be classified as idols instead of heroes. Idols are manmade role models who focus on themselves or a form of worldliness, while heroes are individuals who have integrity and good character. Your child's heroes should be godly adults. You must also select the right movies, music, artists, Websites, television shows, and so forth for your child. Children are not capable of sifting through all of the hype and advertising that is produced by Hollywood and making a right choice.

Help your children recognize the teachers, relatives, neighbors, church leaders, celebrities, and friends who will have the most positive spiritual impact on their lives. Help them to distinguish the real from the false and to realize that popularity does not always determine who has the best character.

Select a good parenting team to help you. Who is having the most influence on your child's life? Other people besides parents have tremendous influence, positive or negative, in a child's life. Search through the godly influencers in your child's life. These may be teachers, pastors, relatives, coaches, neighbors, or family friends. Tell each one how special he or she is in your child's life and how much you appreciate him or her. Ask them to help you accomplish some of the goals you have for your child and to communicate with you what they see happening in your child's life. On separate occasions invite each one to your home for dinner so that your child can have a special time with him or her. This also can be a demonstration of your appreciation to this special person. If your child does not have enough godly influences in his life, then I encourage you to start developing a spiritual parenting team.

Pray for your children by name. God loves your children more than you do. He cares what happens in their lives. Prayer is a time for you to praise God and seek His guidance for your life and the lives of others. God will not only work in the lives of your children, but He will also work in your life. Humble yourself before God each day and pray for each of your children by name.

Use Scripture. The more you read and memorize Scripture, the more you will be able to use it in your daily life. Look for opportunities to discuss with your children what God's Word says. When they are old enough to read and memorize Scripture, encourage them to do so. Better yet, memorize it with them.

Parents have such an important responsibility in the spiritual training of their children.

I have been reminded many times that God is perfect, and we are not. God has a plan for each of our lives. It is a journey. It is one step at a time. It is a growth process. We tend to be impatient. "Just give me salvation, God; I don't have time for the other stuff" is what we say to God by the way we live. Our children are much too precious for us to miss the opportunity God gives us with them. Parenting is not always convenient, but it is a commitment. Leading your children to Christ involves more than a ten-minute lesson at bedtime. Spiritual birth is a process just like physical birth is. Parents who fail to see this fail to understand Scripture and ultimately fail as parents. Churches fail too when they are only concerned with evangelism and not discipleship. This gives the message that numbers are more important than people are. Jesus concerned Himself with both of these principles, because they go together.

The Struggle We Face

What are some of the biggest mistakes that parents make? More important, how do we avoid them? We all make mistakes, but the mature Christian learns from his mistakes and seeks to grow as a result. Here are some common mistakes parents make.

- Expecting each of our children to respond the same to the gospel. Every child is unique in the way he learns, reacts, and behaves.
- Waiting until our children come to us before beginning spiritual training.
- Expecting the church to take the responsibility as the spiritual leader of our children.
- Not using the team God has put around our children (grandparents, teachers, neighbors, and Christian friends).
- Failing to be the godly examples that we should be. Talk is cheap.

- Using symbolic, churchy, religious terms that don't make sense to children without explanation. We treat our children like little adults and assume that they are on the same spiritual level as we are.

A child may not want to brush his teeth, but he does not get to choose whether he does or not. It is part of his daily routine. Good parents will make sure that their children brush their teeth. Hopefully, when those children become adults, living in their own homes, away from their parents, they will continue this important, healthful habit.

Leading a child to become a Christian is not the same as teaching a child to brush his teeth. He will have to make the decision for Christ himself. You cannot do it for him, as much as you would like to do so. You get to teach him to love and obey God, and hopefully he will want to give God control of his life. You can teach him the steps for becoming a Christian, but he will have to take those steps himself. You need to provide an atmosphere that will cause your child to want to become a Christian. Helping your child become a Christian does involve your demonstrating and requiring good Christian habits. Adults are blessed to get to walk alongside these little lambs before, during, and after they decide to follow Christ. What an awesome responsibility, privilege, and joy that is.

The struggle seems to be between how much the parent should initiate and how much the child should initiate. This dilemma causes parents much agony and, many times, fear. It is the most important event in their child's life, and no parent on earth wants to blow it.

Dozens of moms who have brought their kids to visit my office have explained their struggle in this way: "Jonathan has begun asking about becoming a Christian. I really don't think he is fully ready, but I don't know what to tell him. I am also afraid that if something were to happen to him and he was killed I would not know that he is going to heaven." Though God has commanded us to take our Christian parenting seriously, He does not want us to struggle, agonize, or worry. Most of the time when children first begin to ask about becoming a Christian they are really saying, "I am interested," not "I am ready." The key is knowing the difference.

Most of the parents and teachers I know really love their children. But in my own life I have found that *loving children is only the beginning step in leading children to Christ.* That alone does not qualify us to be effective witnesses to children. You must learn how children think. You must study your child. You must look past the outside and try to see your child as God does.

Children are our little lambs, and we must feed them and lead them. And this takes time. That means you need to be involved in your child's spiritual journey before, during, and after he is ready to accept Christ. This definitely calls for patience, commitment, and sensitivity. Being a parent isn't easy, is it? Being a children's Sunday school teacher isn't either. But God knows that and will give us wisdom and strength if we ask Him.

Parental Stumbling Blocks

There seem to be *three major stumbling blocks* in our lives that have a negative impact on our children's decision to accept Christ.

Our ignorance. We do not know as much about the Bible or about children as we should. Wisdom comes from knowledge, experience, and seeking God's help. We live in a world that puts a lot of emphasis on feelings. We should not depend solely on how we feel about things when leading a child to Christ. We must be informed, knowledgeable, sensitive, and wise.

Our inconsistency. We are not as faithful in our daily walk or example as we need to be. We may not feel we have all the right words to say when talking to children about the Lord, but if our walk with the Lord is inconsistent we can know all the right words to say and it will not matter. Hypocrisy will confuse and greatly discourage children. A parent who has a consistent walk with the Lord builds a strong and stable foundation in his child's life.

Our impurity. Our sin is a stumbling block. We allow sin to dwell in us, making us insensitive to the Holy Spirit's leadership. The sin in our lives leaves us powerless as Christians and parents. It takes away our spiritual effectiveness.

If we do not deal with these three areas, we will surely be a stumbling block to our precious children. Are you a stumbling block or a stepping stone? Are you willing to make the effort to be the spiritual leader in your child's life?

THE ROLE TEACHERS HAVE IN LEADING CHILDREN TO CHRIST

The Major Role of the Christian Teacher

What would parents do without the dedicated team of teachers who invest in their child's education and Christian development? Many boys and girls decide to accept Jesus Christ as their personal Savior because of the influence of their teacher(s).

For those of you who touch the lives of children as teachers, I join all parents in saying "thanks." Maybe you are a Sunday school teacher, a school teacher, a vacation Bible school volunteer, a camp counselor, an altar counselor, or a church staff member. If so, you have a mighty impact on the spiritual lives of boys and girls.

Children's Sunday school teachers and Christian school teachers have become the spiritual surrogate parents for many of today's young people. You may not be with each child when he rises up each morning or goes to bed at night, but you are definitely a special part of the journey as you *sit* with him and *walk along the way* with him through his young life. You may be the only one doing any significant spiritual training in that child's life. Believe me, when it comes to building a child's faith, you are a valuable part of the construction team.

You have many of the same opportunities to influence children that we've addressed earlier in this chapter. Largely because of your limited time with the children, you also have some chances to make mistakes that are unique to your position.

121

Some of the Mistakes Teachers Can Make

Not spending enough individual time with the children. Elementary teachers are some of the least appreciated professionals in our society. They are also some of the most committed individuals I know. However, because they have to manage an entire class throughout the day, they do not have as much time for individual interaction with students as they would desire. Teachers must do their best to carve out individual time for each student if they want to get to know them and hear from them.

Children's ministry volunteers have the same challenge. Most ministries are understaffed and have little time for giving individual attention to their students. If every Sunday school teacher and vacation Bible school volunteer would take a few minutes each day to spend with an individual child, we would see the number of children who come to Christ greatly increase.

Not following up class presentations or worship services with personal conversations. Christian schools often use chapel services as their sole evangelistic tool. Chapel services can have a wonderful impact in a child's decision (especially when the speaker knows how to relate with kids), but they are not enough. When kids are asked in a group to raise their hands if they want to follow Christ, each one who raised a hand should be privately counseled afterward.

Sunday school teachers have similar opportunities. Immediately following a Bible story, the pastor's sermon, or a special children's program, we should take advantage of those teachable moments. Most churches could do a better job with individual follow-up.

Assuming that every child is at the same spiritual level. We have already discussed how children go through spiritual stages. However, these are only guidelines. A class of third graders will not all be on the same level spiritually. Know your lambs. Discover where they are spiritually. Follow up with appropriate, individual conversations that will encourage them to follow the Lord.

Assuming that your success as a teacher is based on how many "decisions" are made in your class during the year. Once a second-grade teacher stopped me with some good news. He was excited that all but one child in his class had accepted Christ, and he was working on that last one. This teacher had a real heart for children and the Lord. He did not know much about seven-year-olds and did not realize how easily influenced they are. I was thrilled that he wanted to win every child to Christ. The problem was that his methods were inappropriate.

Besides not knowing about how a child's faith develops, he had an inappropriate way of publicly acknowledging each child's decision. Whenever a child in his class made a decision to become a Christian, he would bring the child gifts and present them to the child in front of the class the following week. A better approach might be to privately praise the child for his decision and to have a time of prayer with him. Publicly presenting awards for accepting Christ puts pressure on young children. They may want the gifts more than they want Christ, and it tempts them to make a premature decision. The students also wanted to have the teacher's approval, and obviously, deciding to become a Christian made him happy.

Everyone likes to receive attention, gain affection, or be appreciated. When a child receives Christ it brings out our greatest joy. The problem occurs when teachers or churches publicly award children who have trusted Christ. Every child watching wants the prize and recognition so much that the decision to follow Christ becomes overshadowed. Show your appreciation in a private way that does not tempt the child you are talking with or any children who might observe your actions.

Reacting to pressure. Do not let the expectations of your supervisor or your personal ego pressure you to produce decisions. This should not be your motivation.

Not communicating with parents. Parents can be a teacher's greatest resource. They can help teachers better understand their children. Though many seem far too busy, they do want to know what is going on in their children's lives and to give input.

Parents depend on teachers to provide much of the spiritual

training their children receive. They may not stop long enough to show their appreciation, but it does exist. Parents often complain that teachers do not communicate enough about their children's needs and successes. Parents also feel that the only time they receive communication is when their child misbehaves or has a problem.

Learn the value of communicating with parents. Take time to visit in every home if possible. View the parent/teacher relationship as a team dedicated to raising that child. Involve parents in their children's spiritual life.

Forgetting to give God credit. Teachers always have an answer. If not immediately, they will research until they do. Teachers can give the appearance of not needing God. They can figure things out for themselves. This amazes children. They look to their teacher as the answer to almost everything. Make sure your students know where your truth comes from. Use your influence to point children to the Master Teacher.

Chapter Eight
Children and Baptism

 O ne of the best ways we can strengthen a child's understanding of the gospel is by separating salvation from baptism. Baptism often seems to overshadow salvation, especially in churches with frequent baptisms, and that is so confusing to our children. Many children put more emphasis on the baptism than the salvation experience because it is what they can see.

Many churches and parents, out of fear of holding a child back, allow a child to be baptized the same day he prays or expresses an interest in becoming a Christian. Since most children see baptism as a part of salvation, it is good to separate the two. Baptizing a child before he has had a personal transformation is not biblical.

Please give children enough time to truly experience salvation before you even discuss or consider baptism. I am not recommending that you wait until your child is twelve before he is baptized. Just make sure that he can understand the difference between his salvation and his baptism. Sometimes it is just not obvious whether a child has had a salvation experience. You may not be positive one way or the other. Wait as long as you can so that the child has time to produce evidence that he has truly been saved.

Wait to see if your child expresses a desire to be baptized. Occasionally talk about his decision to become a Christian and the changes that have occurred in his life. After adequate time, if your child has demonstrated a real change, a true conviction of sin, and a genuine faith and he understands the difference between salvation and baptism, then feel free to baptize him. Don't feel pressured to baptize your child until you have had enough time to observe him.

UNDERSTANDING BAPTISM

Our Jewish friends wait until a child is twelve before he is allowed to fully participate in worship. At this time he is presented to the Jewish community. There is wisdom in this. I would recommend that if your young child desires to accept Christ, don't discourage him. Just wait some time before he is allowed to go public. Give him some time to grow. Help him focus on salvation and what that means before he joins the church, is baptized, or participates in the Lord's Supper. Many times these special events happen too quickly after a child's decision to become a Christian and do not give him time to understand, appreciate, and enjoy them.

The Bible does not teach that our job as parents starts when our children reach the age of twelve, though some parents fix on that age. Nor does Scripture teach that our job is over when our children reach the age of twelve. But many times we act as if our spiritual responsibility is finished when our child decides that he wants to become a Christian. We quickly shift to a baptism mode. It is sad when parents act as if their only job as parents is to see that their child gets baptized. You can almost see them spiritually "check out" within a month after the child has been baptized.

We parents don't always know what the proper response

should be. Two problems often occur at the time a child begins to accept Christ:

- baptizing a child too soon after his initial interest in becoming a Christian
- doing very little to help a child grow once he has become a Christian

Our job as parents does not end when our children begin to ask questions about God. It is just beginning. Baptism is not the solution or proper response at this moment. Its effectiveness and purpose will come later. The responsibility for a child's spiritual understanding is on the parents' shoulders, and many do not want it. Some parents are worried about their child's decision and just want to get it over with. Others put the responsibility on the church and do not get involved. Some use their child's decision as a time to receive public recognition.

Baptism is an act of obedience, a very important act of obedience. However, it is not the only act of obedience, and children need time to understand and show signs of maturity before they are baptized. Give children the positive recognition and support they need at the time of their salvation. Then revisit that experience when they get baptized. That gives you two opportunities to spiritually encourage your child while providing the growth he needs between the two.

INFANT BAPTISM OR INFANT BLESSING?

Segments of the church have misunderstood the story of Jesus in the tenth chapter of Mark when He "took the children in his arms . . . and blessed them." They have used this to support their practice of infant baptism. If Jesus wanted us to observe infant baptism He would have told us. Jesus blessed these children; He did not baptize them.

What is wrong with baptizing infants or young children? Won't baptism help young children prepare to become Christians later? No. The Bible says that we must first repent of our sins before being baptized (Acts 2:38; 3:19). Infant baptism is based more on the covenant that parents are making than the child's own personal commitment to Christ. Baptism was never intended as a promise of things to come. It is a public confession of the personal repentance that has already taken place in a person's life. Many children are being raised to think that this act of baptism alone saves from sin. But the Bible does not teach that.

Your church may practice infant baptism (or some form of dedication service) for the purpose of allowing a child's parents to make a covenant before God. You may want to participate in that type of service. But do not teach your child to equate that dedication service as the equivalent of his own personal baptism that will come later.

Baptism is not the same as a blessing. Baptism is a public confession of faith. Giving children a public blessing is a wonderful idea. It can be a very touching and powerful occasion for all who attend. Many churches do this through parent/baby dedication services. At this time the church recognizes the new baby, parents, and family. Usually, a pastor will publicly ask the parents to commit themselves to being godly parents and then pray for the child and parents by name. This should be a time for the parents to publicly dedicate themselves, their child, and their homes to the Lord.

God honors these special prayer services; however, a baby dedication service is more of a wake-up call for the parents and the church, not for the baby. This is not a time for babies to make a commitment but for parents to commit themselves to raising their child to know the Lord. It is a time for parents to say, "I will teach my child and live a life that will point my child toward Christ." We should not confuse the commitment a person makes when he or she becomes a parent with the commitment a person makes when he or she is being baptized.

We should look for ways and times to bless our young children. To bless means to make encouraging comments to them or say a prayer for them. We should pray for and encourage our children. These may be the greatest influences in our children's decision to accept Christ.

PROPER TIMING OF BAPTISM

Baptism is often a sign of completion to a child. If handled incorrectly, it tends to say to the child and parent, "You have done everything now; you are finished." Baptism should not be used as a type of spiritual closure.

Baptism should also never be used as a status symbol. If a child (or parent) has the attitude "I have arrived" or "look at me," then he is not ready for baptism. Baptism is an act of humility, submission, obedience, and celebration.

Parents should not be pressured or feel bad because their friends' children are being baptized. There should be no race or competition to see whose children are baptized first. We should each desire God's timing for our children. It is good to have a spiritual team that will give us advice about our children. Relatives, friends, teachers, coaches, and pastors can also help as we look for signs of spiritual maturity in our children.

What should you tell a child who wants to be baptized if you feel he is not ready? "Just like God planned your birthday, He also has planned your baptism day. Be patient, and spend the next few months growing and learning. He will let us know when it is the right time. You *will* be baptized. God is preparing you for it. Baptism is one way of showing your obedience to God. But it is not the only way of showing obedience. God is still showing you what it means to be a Christian. One day He will show you what it means to be baptized. I am here to help you. Thank you for wanting to obey God with your life."

The church must decide what it will do about *children and baptism*. Parents and children both need help with this. The church should decide what ages it will baptize and what ages it will not baptize. It may want to handle each child on a case-by-case basis and not have a firm policy regarding age. But formulating some type of age guidelines will help the parents and teachers in your church. It will also help your pastor in his approach to meeting with children. Churches have a variety of beliefs about baptism. Some churches baptize babies, while others wait until the child is twelve. Other churches have no baptism guidelines at all. Churches should give parents (and children) clear guidelines on how they baptize children.

As a general rule, I recommend that you not baptize children who are younger than seven and a half years old or under second grade. Most children younger than that have not actually accepted the Lord. The Bible never specifically mentions children being baptized. It only mentions the baptism of men and women and households, which may or may not have included children. We know that children attended sermons. But we do not know whether they were baptized.

PREPARATION FOR BAPTISM

You and your child should meet with the pastor prior to your child's baptism. The purpose of this visit is not only to evaluate the child's needs and to prepare him for baptism; it is also a time of encouragement, explanation, and celebration for the child. This is also an opportunity for you and your child to build a good relationship with the pastor. If possible, the child should meet with the pastor who will be baptizing him.

Before you begin discussing the baptism, the pastor will probably take a few minutes privately to make sure that the child has already become a Christian. If the child is not quite sure about his salvation, the pastor may review the steps of salvation. When the pastor asks your child questions, be sure not to dominate the discussion or answer for the child.

The pastor will explain what will happen during baptism. He may tell the child that this will be a good time for him to give a verbal testimony. If the pastor will ask the child questions during the baptism, ask him to tell you and the child what he will ask so your child can be prepared. If he wants the child to prepare a short testimony, he will tell him that. Here are a few suggestions of what that testimony might include:

- State your name and age.
- Tell when and where you accepted Christ. Give a few details.

- Thank those who influenced you.
- Quote a favorite Scripture verse.
- Ask the church to pray for you.

Tell the child to write it out; then he should memorize it and place it in a clear plastic bag. After the child has given his testimony the pastor will usually say some things to him and the church, then baptize him.

During the meeting with the pastor, the pastor will probably

- physically practice the baptism (where to stand, bend knees, hold nose);
- discuss the time and place to meet, and what to wear;
- remind you to think about whom you want to invite;
- give guidelines about photography before and during baptism; and
- end with a time of prayer, in which each person prays, including the child.

The pastor may also spend some time discussing steps of Christian growth with your child, or he may recommend that the child attend a discipleship class for children. In the next chapter we'll look at some ways the church can help disciple children. But your job does not decrease in importance if your church does a good job discipling children. You and your spouse will always be the most important people in discipling your child.

Before you leave his office, take a photo of the pastor and the child.

Consider hosting a post-baptism party in honor of this special occasion. You can ask those present to give a Scripture or prayer specifically for the child. Gifts are optional. Ask the child to give a testimony. In addition to family, friends, and neighbors, the pastor and child's teachers should also be included.

Chapter Nine
Children and Discipleship: The Church's Role

*A*ll through this book, I've been talking primarily to parents. In this chapter, I'd like to shift the focus a bit and talk to pastors, teachers, and children's ministry leaders. If you are a parent, you can still learn something from this chapter as we examine the church's role in the life of a child who is a new believer.

HOW DOES A DISCIPLESHIP RELATIONSHIP START?

When parents bring a child to you for discipleship or the child expresses interest in baptism or church membership, the first thing to do is determine whether the child is actually saved. Ask him to tell you about when he accepted the Lord. If the child has not made a personal decision to accept Christ, ask him to do so right there or to go home and discuss it with his parents and pray with them.

On several occasions I have discovered that the child I am talking to is spiritually mature but does not recall personally praying to trust the Lord. If you face such a situation (the child's parents recall a time that he has trusted Christ, but the child does not have a strong memory of it), you can allow the child to pray again to settle the issue. If he expresses faith in Christ and his parents are sure of his salvation, but he just can't tell you a specific time, pray with the child and together thank the Lord for his salvation. In either case, ask the parents to join you.

The Bible teaches that two of the functions of the church (two ways to grow a church) are to *reach* people (evangelism) and to *raise* people (discipleship). Parenting and children's ministries are especially rewarding because they involve both evangelism and discipleship. Leading a child to accept Christ does not mean that we have completed our assignment. Our next responsibility is to disciple the new Christian. So many children who have joyously given their lives to Jesus are then left alone to wither away because no one takes the responsibility to disciple them in their faith. Churches sometimes put more emphasis on getting children to make *decisions* than helping them become solid Christians *(disciples)*. See the difference? It takes about ten minutes to lead a child to make a decision and about ten years to grow a disciple.

WHAT IS THE ROLE OF THE DISCIPLER?

What are our responsibilities in winning and discipling children for Christ? The following terms describe our multiple roles:

> **Builder** (Encourager): Designer
> **Archer** (Teacher): Marksman, Guide
> **Fisherman** (Evangelist): Casting the net,
>   Drawing the net
> **Shepherd** (Discipler): Protector, Provider

Children are like wet clay in a potter's hands. They are so easily shaped and fashioned into any design we desire. Once the clay is allowed to sit, exposed to the elements, it is much harder to shape. It has already taken on a shape of its own. Children who are not discipled while they are young believers can grow up to be weak or hardened Christians. They eventually have to be broken in order for God to continue shaping their lives.

We had better wake up and realize that we are not doing a good job leading our kids to Christ. The bad news is that we are doing a worse job discipling them. We must become more deliberate at passing our faith on to the next generation. Getting our kids baptized at an early age does not mean we have succeeded or completed the job.

A child's salvation is only the beginning. Once that seed has been planted and takes root, it is time to feed, water, and care for the plant.

WHAT CAN A CHURCH TEACH YOUNG CHRISTIANS?

Once a child has taken the step of faith and become a new believer, what should we do to help him grow? How can we help him develop into a strong young Christian?

Ephesians 6:10–18 says,

Be strong in the Lord and in his mighty power. Put on the full armor of God so that you can take your stand against the devil's schemes. For our struggle is not against flesh and blood, but against the rulers, against the authorities, against the powers of this dark world and against the spiritual forces of evil in the heavenly realms. Therefore put on the full armor of God, so that when the day of evil comes, you may be able to stand your ground, and after you have done everything, to stand. Stand firm then, with the belt of truth buckled around your waist, with the breastplate of righteousness in place, and with your feet fitted with the readiness that comes from the gospel of peace. In addition to all this, take up the shield of faith, with which you can extinguish all the flaming arrows of the evil one. Take the helmet of salvation and the sword of the Spirit, which is the word of God. And pray in the Spirit on all occasions with all kinds of prayers and requests.

This Scripture teaches us how a Christian dresses for success.

When a child is young, his parents have to dress him each day. When he gets older he learns to do it for himself. Until a child can spiritually dress himself, we must do it for him. Satan attacks young Christians as soon as he can. We must prepare them. We must protect them. The first step we take after a child accepts the Lord is to teach him how to grow, get stronger, and trust God's protection. Just as an athlete trains to compete and win, so should Christians. What are some things we should teach a child who is a new Christian? Here are a few:

- How to pray
- How to study the Bible
- How to repent of personal sin
- How to witness
- How to handle money and the tithe
- How to handle trials and temptation
- How to build friendships
- The importance of church life

A new believer particularly needs to understand important daily habits, like worship, prayer, and Scripture reading. He also needs to understand the Christian life in a deeper sense: respecting and loving others, witnessing for Christ, obeying Christ, repentance and forgiveness. And he needs to understand his place in the church body.

Talk with the child about spending time with God each day through prayer and Bible reading. Prayer should be a time of praise, confession, praying for others, and asking for guidance. Bible reading should include one story (complete subject or paragraph) at a time. You might want to give him a resource that will guide him in what to read. With an older child, you can suggest that he keep a daily journal. After he has read Scripture, he can discuss it with his parents or write what he has learned in his journal.

Relationships are an important part of the Christian life. The child should begin to be deliberate about how he relates to others. His parents are his best friends until he gets married. They are the most significant authority God has placed in his life and his main teachers. Schoolteachers and Sunday school teachers also have a God-given position in his life. As he gets older, friends will have a greater influence on his life. He should learn the balance of loving everyone but choosing the right friends.

Discuss with the child the meaning of different elements of the church service, including the purpose of the Lord's Supper. It is a time of personal evaluation, a private confession time with the Lord, a time of remembrance of what Jesus did on the cross, and a time of celebration with the body of believers. Help him to understand what the church provides that will help him to grow. Give him suggestions of what he can offer the church even now (praying, greeting visitors, being helpful to younger children, giving, worshiping with others, etc.). Answer any questions he may have.

Help him to think about how he is growing and how he still needs to grow. Help him to think about the choices he is making and to determine to make good choices in the future.

WAYS A CHURCH CAN REACH FAMILIES WITH CHILDREN

There seem to be at least *five times when unchurched families are more receptive* to the church. You will notice that most involve their children. Each of these events is an open door for the church to present the Good News. How the church responds at these special times will leave a long-lasting impact.

When a Child Is Born

The birth of a child can cause the most godless parent to stop and take inventory of his or her life. Responsibilities change when one becomes a parent. Life is usually taken a bit more seriously. The thought of raising a child can be very scary and draws parents to seek help from others. Every parent wants his child to be loved, happy, well-adjusted, and well behaved. The church can and should be a place that is well equipped and respected in helping with this task.

I once visited an unchurched couple who just had a new baby boy. When I arrived the father, a truck driver, was outside working on his truck. He was under the hood with grease up to his elbows. I knew that I had caught him at an inconvenient time. When I introduced myself and told him I was there to meet his new son, his face lit up and he said, "Just a minute; I'll be right back." In a few minutes he returned, all clean, with his new son in his giant arms. As he stuck out the baby for me to get a better look, he said, "I want you to meet my son." He was beaming. When a baby enters a home it can soften the hearts of the toughest men, and God will use that to introduce men and women to the heavenly Father's love. I will never forget that father's face.

Churches that welcome newborns in their community make a statement to parents. They are saying that babies are very special to the church family and to God. Parents get the message that the church is available to help them raise this gift from God. They also are reminded of the importance of being the best parents they can be and encouraged that the church can help them.

When a Child Starts School

When a child leaves home to face the world alone it can be a frightening time for a parent. "Is my child ready for school? How will he face the pressures of the world? Will he make friends? Will he face bullies? Will he miss me? Will he be lonely? What type of teacher will he have? Will he like his teacher more than me? Will he be exposed to things that will hurt him emotionally or morally? Have I done a good job as a parent to prepare him? Will he make good choices? Will he be a leader or a crowd follower? What school is best for my child? Should we choose a Christian school instead of a public school?" These are just a few of the questions parents ask themselves when their child is about to begin school. Many parents want to get their children baptized before they start school. They feel as if this will inoculate them against the evil they will face.

When a Child Has Personal Problems

Children today are faced with a myriad of personal problems. These may be the result of emotional strain, stress, learning challenges, and pressure from the world around them. When children hurt, so do those children's parents. If the church will address these hurts and help parents know what to do when they face painful situations, it will build relationships with parents and children.

Many churches have support groups for children and parents who have gone through divorce, have experienced abuse, have trouble dealing with anger, live in a blended family, live with an alcoholic or drug user, etc.

When a Teenager Is Rebelling

Not all teens rebel, but most struggle as they face making tougher choices, dealing with peer pressure, and discovering their identity. It may be too late to reach a particular rebellious teenager, but only God knows for sure, and it is not too late to try. Parents desperately want our love and support during tough times such as this. Sometimes parents will blame the church for their child's rebellion, and they may be bitter toward the church. They also may be angry toward God. But most parents are receptive to love. The church that understands and reaches out to teens will win the hearts of parents as well.

When There Is a Medical Emergency or Death in the Family

Death brings pain to those loved ones who are left behind. This pain can be healed with the peace and love we receive from Jesus. Families need the Lord and the church during this time. Most families will be receptive to and appreciative of our acts of kindness and compassion during their time of grief.

HOW CAN A CHURCH REACH
CHILDREN FOR CHRIST?

Define the Purpose of Its Children's Ministry

The church must first *define the purpose* of its children's ministry. Second, it must set goals that will help it accomplish the purpose. Third, a church will have to choose activities that will help reach these goals. This will most likely involve making some changes in the current activities in order to upgrade and improve the overall children's ministry. For some churches a total restructuring will need to take place.

The basic elements of a healthy children's ministry might include Bible study, evangelism, fellowship, and discipleship. It must be fun. It must be biblical. It must involve the children. It must be age appropriate.

Many churches act as if the purpose of children's programs is to provide free, quality child care while parents enjoy the church activities. Children's ministry can be so much more than simply "child care."

Develop a Strategy for Reaching Children

If a church does not provide quality children's activities for the parents who are on campus, those parents will not stay long. *Today's parents demand quality care* for their children. However, children's ministry of this century will have to be much more than the *child care* of the past century if churches plan to reach young families. Churches are going to have to get out of the *baby-sitting* business and get into the *child-building* business. There is a great void in children's ministry in the church. Families are searching for a church that steps up to the plate and puts children's ministry as one of its choice priorities.

How do churches move *from a child-care mentality* to a *child outreach mentality?* They must see children's ministry as a key part of the church's strategy for reaching non-Christians. Churches must realize that a dynamic children's ministry is a key to reaching today's family. It can be one of the greatest outreach tools of the church.

Churches should focus on (1) *reaching new families* and (2) *growing the families that they have.* A strong children's ministry will do both. Build a children's ministry that is a reaching and equipping center for kids. Design a children's ministry that will become both a spiritual haven for kids and a place they will want to bring their friends.

The church must ask, "Are we going to evangelize children? If so, how will we do it?"

There are only two choices. You can be reactive or proactive. To be reactive you just respond as the needs (or problems) arise. To be proactive you lead the church to provide guidelines for parents, children, and children's leaders that will encourage them to know how to lead their children to Christ.

Here are some guidelines to consider regarding children and evangelism.

Do not rely solely on the mass evangelism approach as your vehicle for leading children to Christ. It has its place and can be very effective. It is easy to persuade children to respond at an event (VBS, camp, Sunday school rally, etc.), especially if the speaker or entertainer is appealing or convincing. Using this type of event occasionally is a good balance. Once or twice a year is probably enough. Events that include large groups of children can give focus, inspiration, encouragement, reminders, etc. They can be a wonderful time of worship, teaching, fun, and evangelism. They should avoid pressuring or manipulating children through scare tactics, fear, or heavy emotional pleas. Special events are excellent times for children to bring their unchurched friends. If children are encouraged to accept Christ at one of these special events, make plans to personally talk to each child who responds.

Some of the most effective evangelism with children is *through one-on-one relationships with their parents and teachers.* Train your children's parents, leaders, and volunteers how to witness to children. Teach them the principles you have learned in this book, and help them set times when they will talk with their children about salvation. Sometimes we think that a good Bible lesson is all a child needs. God uses His Word to penetrate our hearts and the hearts of children. But He also uses our personal witness.

Don't assume that because a child attends a Bible study class at church (or attends a Christian school) that he has been fully evangelized. Every child needs someone to take a personal interest in his spiritual life. Each child needs someone to lead him to Jesus, not just tell him about Jesus. Train teachers to spend individual time with the children they influence.

Children who are age seven and under should not be pushed to accept Christ. Most are not ready to make that decision final. Too much pressure is being put on children at this age to "make a decision now." Instead, they need to be encouraged to start thinking about being a Christian. If a child insists on becoming a Christian at such a young age, what should you do? You can say to him, "If you want to become a Christian now that is fine, but we are going to wait until later for you to be baptized so you will have plenty of time to grow and understand what that means."

For older children, you should *be more specific* with them about the decision to become a Christian. Make it simple, make it personal, do not pressure, let them know what to do, and offer to help them if they need it. Talk one-on-one with every child who makes a decision. Then follow up with each child and his parents.

Train and ask each teacher in the children's ministry to *privately discuss* with each child what it means to be a Christian. Young children need to hear what it means to be a Christian and be given the time to think about it and understand it. Older children (age eight and older) need to be encouraged to make this decision with their lives and personally approached about doing so. Without pressuring the child, once you feel that he understands, ask him what he wants to do. If he is ready to commit his life to Christ, lead him through the steps of becoming a Christian (see pages 104–105). Be sure to inform or include the child's parents. Follow up to make sure he is being discipled, getting established in his daily habits, and becoming active in church activities for his age.

Occasionally remind the church to *invite families with unchurched children* to attend. Some churches have outreach programs such as bus ministry, backyard Bible clubs, or other activities for children. But just think of the impact it would make if Christians would begin to invite their neighbors (or the children in the neighborhood) to ride to church with them each Sunday.

Train and encourage the children who do attend to *invite their friends*. This should be part of the children's ministry philosophy. Give them special days to help highlight the importance of reaching their friends.

Teach Children How to Witness

Plan and host *community events* that attract children. These serve as entry points for unchurched families that are less threatening than Sunday can be. These also give members something to which they can invite their friends. Events might include a fall festival, children's day, vacation Bible school, movie premiers, concerts, or special guests.

Beyond that, help your children understand how to present the gospel and how to talk to their friends about Jesus. Help them learn how to explain some good Scripture verses. Give them a tool they can use as they witness to their friends and classmates.

Develop a Strategy for Producing Leaders

The church must *produce leaders and volunteers* who have a passion for children's ministry. This is one of the biggest challenges of today's church. Churches all over the land are being crippled due to a lack of leadership in their children's ministry, especially in their programs for younger children. Enlistment should not be the job of one person. Those who oversee the children's ministry of the church need to spend most of their time leading and equipping their leaders. Most spend far too much time enlisting and not enough time equipping, creating, evaluating, designing, etc. The church must send its little lambs enough leaders and volunteers so they will be properly taught and cared for. No church will succeed at effective children's ministry unless it successfully addresses and solves the problem of leadership and volunteer enlistment. This is a church-wide responsibility.

Develop a Strategy for Providing Resources

The church must *provide enough money and resources* to get the job done. This can be done through budgeting each year and special offerings. Adults tend to spend more on themselves and overlook the ministries to children. Have a budget that says reaching and discipling children are a priority. Young families that you reach through the children's ministry may not come from a background of tithing and giving. However, parents will give to ministries that have a positive impact on their kids. Those who do not have children will also give if they can see how their gifts will touch the lives of the church's little ones.

Decide How to Care for Children Who Are Becoming Christians

Develop a process that will assist children who are becoming Christians and their parents. When a child begins to accept Christ the church should be there for him with *outstretched arms.* The child should have his parents holding one hand and his church holding the other. Sometimes the church has to hold both hands of the child because there is no parental support. The reverse is also true. Parents must be prepared to take full spiritual responsibility when the church does not have a ministry in place to assist children during this time.

What are some specific steps that churches should take to assist children and parents?

Train the young parents of the church how to be good parents. In most churches this is the missing key to effective children's ministry. No church program can take the place of the parent. Parents are the primary shapers of their child's adult personality. Here is a sample of topics that should be included in a parent training class:

- What the Bible says about children

- How to have a godly home
- The role of today's father
- The role of today's mother
- How to be a successful parent
- How to effectively discipline your child
- How to build character in your child
- How to build a strong relationship with your child
- How to love your child
- How to build self-confidence in your child
- How to lead your child to Christ
- How to discover your child's learning style
- How to understand your child's personality
- How to budget your time
- How to budget your money
- How to give your child good memories
- How to give your child good habits
- Resources that are available for parents

Train Parents, Children's Ministry Leaders, and Children's Counselors

Provide training so that those who work with children can understand children and salvation and how to lead children to Christ. Include topics that have been covered earlier in this book (e.g., the stages of spiritual development, the signs that a child is ready to accept Christ, the signs that a child is not ready to accept Christ, how to witness to children, etc.). When the various groups that minister to children are all on the same page philosophically, the ministry to children is strengthened.

Reach Out to Children Who Express an Interest in Knowing Christ

Know how to respond to children when they begin to desire or inquire about becoming a Christian. Have each child meet with a counselor. Counselors should be hand-picked and available on Sundays and/or during the week.

Make an appointment for the child and his parents to come to the church office. Meet with the parents and the child. If the child is ready, encourage him to go to the new believer's class before he is baptized. If the child is not ready, encourage him to keep listening to what his parents, teachers, and pastor are teaching him.

Provide a New Believer's Class for Children Who Have Accepted Christ

Children should be in the second grade or older in order to attend a new believer's class. This should be required prior to baptism. Some churches design the class to help the children with their decision to become a Christian.

Four weeks should be long enough. Classes can include topics such as "Who is Jesus?" "Why is the Bible so important?" "What does our church believe (doctrine, history)?" "What next? How to keep growing," and "Baptism and the Lord's Supper."

Teach Your Church to Be "Child Friendly"

Adults should be encouraged to greet the children they see in the hallways and those who sit close to them during the worship time. It is good for them to hug or touch the children who are within your reach, look children in the eye when speaking to them, and smile at the children when they are speaking or looking at them.

Upgrade your facilities to let children and parents know that this place loves and understands children. Decorate the children's rooms attractively and appropriately. Their appearance should say "We are having fun here; come check us out."

Have an annual "Children's Day" that highlights the children's ministry. Do something special that day for every child. Thank every children's worker who serves in this area. Inform the church about the purpose, success, and needs of this ministry. This should be a day that touches the heart of the church and reminds it of the blessing that children are to the church.

Familiarize the Church and Community with Your Ministry

Create a greater visibility of the children's ministry around the church campus. Place visuals or multimedia presentations in areas that are most traveled and in the areas where parents gather.

Use every opportunity to inform the church and community of programs and ministries that are available through the church and of the fact that children are special and very important to your church and to God. You can use printed materials, posters, mail, and multimedia.

Notify the elementary schools in your community that you are available to help children and parents who need encouragement, counseling, or help. Communicate in a contemporary fashion that you address the needs of today's child and parents.

Keep the Bible as a basis for all that you do. Be clear about how important and reliable the Bible is without cramming it down the throats of those who are still inquiring or seeking.

Host programs or events for parents and children that are open and attractive to the general public and that are nonthreatening.

As you put a proper priority on your children's ministry, children, parents,   and volunteers will become stronger in their relationship with Christ. Remember, Jesus said, "Whoever welcomes a little child . . . in my name welcomes me" (Matthew 18:5).

Moody Press, a ministry of Moody Bible Institute,
is designed for education, evangelization, and edification.
If we may assist you in knowing more about Christ
and the Christian life, please write us without obligation:
Moody Press, c/o MLM, Chicago, Illinois 60610.